Growing in Grace & Wisdom

A Hands-On Religion Resource

Catholic Heritage Curricula
1-800-490-7713   www.chcweb.com

Credits

Cover image: Sieger Köder, Mandelzweig. Katholische Gemeinde Deutscher Sprache, Paris © Sieger Köder-Stiftung Kunst und Bibel, Ellwangen

Interior images: pg. i: © Daria Ustiugova / Shutterstock; pg. iii: St. Joseph © Anne Simoneau; pgs. iii, 1, 3, 13, 19, 24, 29, 35, 39, 51, 63, 75, 89, 99, 103, 106, 109, 115, 124: © Wenpei / Shutterstock; pg. 8-top: Jan Sapák, CC BY-SA 4.0, https://commons.wikimedia.org/w/index.php?curid=48039177; pg. 9-top: Renata Sedmakova / Shutterstock; pg. 9-bottom: Distant Shores Media/Sweet Publishing, CC BY-SA 3.0, https://commons.wikimedia.org/w/index.php?curid=18897593; pg. 11: © Klara Viskova / Shutterstock; pg. 15: © serdjophoto / Shutterstock; pg. 16: © Paul Atkinson / Shutterstock; pgs. 17–18-background: © Bent Chang / Shutterstock; pg.20: © Snova/ Shutterstock; pg. 22: © xbrchx / Shutterstock; pg. 23: © Le Panda / Shutterstock; pg. 26: © AnneMarie Johnson; pg. 27: © helgafo / Shutterstock; pg. 28: © Zic Schrab / Shutterstock; pg. 32-background: © edel / Shutterstock; pgs. 32, 33: recipe card-top: © udra11 / Shutterstock; pgs. 32, 33: recipe card-bottom: © Kraphix / Shutterstock; pg. 38-top: © Iana Alter / Shutterstock; pg. 38-bottom: © Lyudmila Tetera / Shutterstock; pg. 51: Asurnipal, CC BY-SA 4.0, https://commons.wikimedia.org/w/index.php?curid=60759212; pg. 53: https://wellcomeimages.org/indexplus/obf_images/9b/92/e1710d001c13e6f58a8fff0af792.jpg, CC BY 4.0, https://commons.wikimedia.org/w/index.php?curid=36358202; pg. 57: Geobia, CC BY-SA 4.0, https://commons.wikimedia.org/w/index.php?curid=37534975; pg. 72-border: © justaa / Shutterstock; pg. 73-map: © dikobraziy / Shutterstock; pg. 74: © qpiii / Shutterstock; pg. 82: © luna1 / Shutterstock; pg. 85: © Valerii_M / Shutterstock; pg. 87: © GarryKillian / Shutterstock; pg. 97-background: © arikProst / Shutterstock; pg. 97-jar: © gomolach / Shutterstock; pg. 97-heart: © str33t cat / Shutterstock; pg. 106: © Suzanne Tucker / Shutterstock; pg. 107: © Dan Race / Shutterstock; pg. 115: Joannaczopowicz, CC BY-SA 3.0, https://commons.wikimedia.org/w/index.php?curid=2789055; pg. 117: Bundesarchiv, Bild 121-0267 / CC-BY-SA 3.0, https://commons.wikimedia.org/w/index.php?curid=5416271; pg. 118: Joachim Schäfer, Copyrighted free use, https://commons.wikimedia.org/w/index.php?curid=35220037; pg. 121: Hynek Moravec, CC BY 3.0, https://commons.wikimedia.org/w/index.php?curid=3199042; pgs. 122-123: © marco-ryan / Shutterstock; pgs. 128, 130, 132, 134, 136, 138, 140, 142, 144, 146, 148: © Rezi Ziatdin / Shutterstock

Any images not mentioned are in the public domain.

Instructional text adapted from a manuscript by Sandra Garant titled "Cultivating Catholic Creativity." © 2000 Sandra Garant. Used with permission.

Stories of the saints on pgs. 3-6, 51-57, 63-71, 83-84, 109-113, and 115-121 written by Elaine Woodfield. Previously published in *Reading Comprehension: Stories of the Saints, Volume I,* © 1997 Catholic Heritage Curricula.

ISBN: 978-1-946207-39-5

Printed by Bookmasters
Ashland, Ohio, USA
April 2020

Catholic Heritage Curricula
1-800-490-7713 *www.chcweb.com*

Table of Contents

The child grew in
size and strength,
filled with wisdom,
and the grace of God
was upon Him.
(Luke 2:40)

Parent Introduction

Growing in Grace & Wisdom begins with an introduction to creativity and why it is important to develop this gift:

Everyone's creativity comes from our Creator. Creativity is one of the ways we reflect God's image.

Many children are highly creative. With a brown towel wrapped around the shoulders, a boy can turn himself momentarily into St. Francis of Assisi. A person can be highly creative and yet never draw or paint a picture. A creative person may never compose music or write a story. Even if you don't see yourself as being creative, you can cultivate creativity in your child and in yourself.

Not all creativity is equally humane. Adults know what matches can do, and we don't have to explore their possibilities. Young children are irresponsible and creative, which is why God made adults.

We adults need to discover creative ways to watch over our children's natural irresponsibility and creativity and to protect them from too much of either.

The ingenuity of a nine-year-old will not be stifled if he is reprimanded for a "clever" but cutting remark to his sister. If he is that clever, he can certainly be encouraged to compliment his sister constructively, which will strengthen the family relationship.

The irresponsible, unknowledgeable, childish creativity can blossom into a responsible, knowledgeable, faithful, and mature creativity.

Growing in Grace & Wisdom is a religion resource designed to help this process of growth in your child through inspirational stories and hands-on activities.

In the *CHC Lesson Plans for Fifth Grade, Growing in Grace & Wisdom* is scheduled two days a week for 21 weeks. The material is self-directed; the student reads the story the first day and completes the activity the next day.

Books and books and books have been written on family life. Our magazines and newspapers are full of alarming articles on the danger of family life crumbling in our days. Psychiatrists, psychoanalysts, and psychologists are busy in research to answer the question "why." Little do they seem to know that this question was answered two thousand years ago by a few words in the Gospel of Luke. There we see the Heavenly Father making this tremendous new foundation, the Christian family, when He sends His Son to the small home in Nazareth. It is absolutely impossible to meditate too much on the hidden life. Just watching Jesus, Mary, and Joseph in their daily routine will do something for us. There is our model, and there is our only remedy. As the saying from the old country has it: If there are more mothers like Mary and more fathers like Joseph, there will be more children like Jesus.

—Maria von Trapp

1

Why should we pay attention to creativity? Isn't creativity something that only artists and musicians have to worry about? True creativity produces something good, in the same way that God created the universe and saw that it was good. The best creativity flows from deep charity. This kind of creativity creates joy and happiness in those around us. Everyone's creativity comes from our Creator. Creativity is one of the ways we reflect God's image. Let's read a story about a saint who used the gift of his creativity to serve his people.

God's Secret Agent

by Elaine Woodfield

Fr. Miguel Pro turned quickly at the corner and walked rapidly down the sidewalk that was filled with shoppers. Moving fast, he threaded his way through the crowd and slipped around another street corner.

"Perhaps I have lost them," he thought to himself. When he was halfway down the street he permitted himself to look back over his shoulder. He sighed, realizing that he was wrong. The police were about fifty yards behind him. He quickened his pace.

Fr. Pro was glad that he was wearing one of his many disguises. His clothes were very shabby. This helped him to blend into crowds better. But as he looked behind, he realized that today he was unable to lose his pursuers in the crowd. They were closing in on him fast.

Then he had an idea. He looked ahead at the people on the sidewalk and spotted a young woman walking by herself. He would have to take a terrible chance that would mean either his life or his death.

What was his chance? It was the girl. She was a complete stranger to him. If she understood

what he wanted her to do, then he would be safe. But if she was a supporter of the new atheistic government, whose police were chasing him, then the result would be disaster for him.

They were coming closer. He had to take a chance. Fr. Miguel walked up to the girl, linked his arm with hers and bending his head near her ear, he whispered, "Help me—I'm a priest!" Would she help?

She looked up at him, smiled broadly, and squeezed his arm fondly as if she was a "girl-friend" who was glad to see her "boyfriend." The girl had understood perfectly! Arm in arm, the "sweethearts" strolled down the street. The girl peeked behind her.

"They have stopped in the middle of the block. They are looking around very puzzled!" she whispered. It worked! The police were looking for a priest in shabby clothes walking alone, but now he had blended completely into the crowd. He walked quickly with the girl until the police were out of sight and thanked her for her help. She had saved his life! She asked only for his priestly blessing, which he gave her. Fr. Pro then went into a house where someone awaited his priestly ministry.

What was Fr. Miguel Pro's crime? Simply being a Catholic priest in Mexico in 1927 was a crime! The new government of revolutionary men had made it so. This government and all those in power wanted nothing better than to destroy completely the Catholic Faith, because these men were Marxist atheists. This means that they did not believe in God and wanted to eliminate all faith in Him so that they could have complete power over the country and all of its people. They did not follow the Ten Commandments, and they made up their own laws that were unfair to all except themselves.

Catholics still needed the sacraments in 1927 in Mexico. Babies needed baptism, children needed to make their First Confession and First Communion. People needed to be confirmed, couples needed to be married by a priest, everyone needed to receive Jesus in Holy Communion, and the dying needed to receive the Anointing of the Sick. Fr. Miguel Pro needed to travel to these people in Mexico City, so he developed many disguises. Sometimes he wore a mechanic's coverall and cap. Other times he wore the traveling clothes of a poor man. Still other times he dressed like a country farmer. He traveled the city on bicycle, said secret Masses in homes, and made sure that all who needed them received the sacraments. He also collected and gave food to the poor. He knew that he was in constant danger of being caught and put to death, but he remembered that Jesus was in constant danger from His enemies, too, and He continued to serve His people. So Fr. Pro did the same, knowing that because he was a priest, he was to be "another Christ."

Fr. Pro told a friend, "If I am ever caught be prepared to ask me for things in Heaven." He joked that he would cheer up any sad saints by doing a Mexican hat dance.

Fr. Miguel Pro was born in 1891. His father was an engineer, and his mother was a very charitable

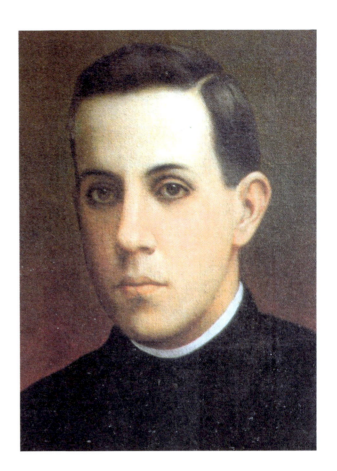

woman. The family was large and close-knit. Young Miguel was known for being a practical jokester. Once when he was taking a walk with one of his sisters, he surprised her by knocking on the door of a house they were passing. A man answered the door.

"Excuse me, sir. My sister was admiring that statue of the Blessed Virgin near your window so much that I wondered if you would sell it to us? My sister has just fallen in love with it," said Miguel all in one breath. His sister was first surprised, then very embarrassed, then tried to make him stop, all to no avail.

"Oh no, young man! I could never sell it—it is our family's treasure!"

Miguel's sister breathed a sigh of relief, then glanced into the man's window. She saw that the statue was not very pretty!

Miguel loved to play guitar for his family in the evenings. Family times were warm, funny, and loving. He prayed about his vocation, and realized that God was calling him to the priesthood. He applied to the Jesuit seminary in 1911.

He was known to be a jokester, even by the staff and students in the seminary. Was he really serious about wanting to be a priest? They tested his sincerity. Miguel arrived for an interview with the rector, or director, of the seminary. He entered the rector's office, and was kept standing for a half hour while the rector read a paper and seemed not to notice him at all! Then all of a sudden he looked up at Miguel and told him to come back again! This happened twice. The third time, as he was waiting, Miguel heard the loud shouts of the seminary students in the nearby courtyard. They were shouting about what an awful place the seminary was. Miguel realized that he was being "tested," and that his calmness helped him pass the "test." His dream came true: he was accepted! Miguel had reason to be grateful for this "test" in later years when his calmness helped to save his life and to help others.

There had started a bloody revolution in Mexico in 1910, and the fighting was coming close to the seminary, so the seminarians had to travel to Europe to complete their studies. Miguel traveled in peasant disguise from Mexico to Texas to California to Nicaragua to Spain to Belgium. He was ordained a priest in 1925, and traveled back to Mexico.

Shortly after he arrived back in his home country, the revolutionary government ordered that all public worship services were now against the law! A person could be arrested for going to Mass! Any priest found would be captured on the spot by the police. So Fr. Pro spent the next two years as a priest secretly serving his people.

He was constantly on the move. He visited a convent one day, and he told the Mother Superior: "I offered my life for the saving of Mexico some time ago, Sister, and this morning at Mass I felt that He accepted it."

In 1927, a bomb was thrown from a car at the revolutionary president, General Calles. The men who threw the bomb were not caught, but the car was. It had belonged to Fr. Pro's brother, Humberto, long ago. He was not involved, and had a strong alibi for the time of the attack, and of course this was also the case for Fr. Pro and their brother, Roberto. None of the Pro brothers were involved in any way in the bomb incident. But General Calles ordered their arrest. The Pro brothers went into hiding. They were betrayed by a boy who was afraid for the life of his mother, captured, and put into prison.

There was no trial. The prisoners were ordered to be executed, or put to death. While in prison, Fr. Pro helped his brothers and the other prisoners to prepare for death. He talked with them and calmed their fears. He prayed with them, and spoke about Heaven, and heard their confessions. Fr. Pro's sister, Anna, tried to get a stay of execution for all three of her brothers. Roberto alone was released.

The day of execution dawned. The policeman who arrested Fr. Pro cried and asked his forgiveness. Fr. Pro gently forgave him, and also forgave the members of the firing squad for what they were going to do. It would be easy to be angry at them for doing something so unfair, but Fr. Pro remembered that Jesus on the cross forgave his enemies.

General Calles was proud of himself for ordering the death of Fr. Pro, and he wanted all of Mexico to see Fr. Pro's execution. So he ordered many newspaper reporters to be present in the courtyard at the execution, and ordered that they take many pictures of it with their cameras. He wanted to make the people afraid to practice their Catholic Faith after seeing that the revolutionary government would put all priests to death.

The prisoners and guards marched out of the prison into the outdoor courtyard. Fr. Pro looked at the wall where so many had already stood and died. The soldier asked him if he had any last request.

"Yes—to pray in order to prepare my soul for death," he replied. Fr. Pro knelt for a few minutes in prayer.

At this very moment Anna was at the gate of the prison with a stay of execution in her hand. The jailer would not believe her, and did not let her in.

Fr. Pro walked to the execution wall, and stood with his arms outstretched in the form of a cross. He shouted, "Viva Cristo Rey!" Which means "Long live Christ the King!" These were his last words.

Anna heard the shots. They seemed to go through her heart, too. She knew that her brother was a martyr for the Faith, and said a grateful prayer of joy through her tears.

The pictures of Fr. Pro's execution were printed in the newspapers. When they saw them, the people of Mexico were not afraid to practice their Faith. Instead, they were proud of Fr. Pro's courageous death, and were determined to practice their Catholic Faith with new courage.

General Calles forbade anyone from attending the funeral of the Pro brothers. He could not keep away the hundreds of people who came to the Pro house all night long to pay their respects to Fr. Miguel and the Pro family. Silently and respectfully, they filed past Fr. Pro's casket. Fr. Pro's father urged his sister to keep from crying.

"Remember, you are in the presence of a saint," he said.

Not all the police in Mexico could keep away the thousands of men, women, and children who came to the funeral. One blind woman who touched Fr. Pro's body was instantly cured! There were many miracles that day. It was as if Fr. Pro was wishing them to be happy that he was with Jesus in Heaven.

And the miracles continue.

A few years after Fr. Pro's death, the government in Mexico changed, and it was no longer against the law to practice the Catholic Faith. Many people thought that Mexico was saved by Fr. Pro offering his life for it.

Fr. Pro was beatified by St. John Paul II on September 25, 1988 and his feast day is November 23.

Photo taken of Fr. Miguel Pro at his execution

Cheer-Up Joke Book

As we learned in the story, Fr. Miguel Pro was known to be a jokester. Do you like jokes? Have you ever heard someone say, "Laughter is the best medicine"? Having a good sense of humor is surely one of God's special gifts! Use the joke pages below to make a little booklet that you can give to a sibling or friend to cheer him up. Cut the pages out and then staple them together to make a booklet. Ask your family members what their favorite jokes are and add them to your booklet on the blank pages provided. Have fun!

A little girl told her mother that the birth of Christ was announced by angels "while shepherds washed their socks by night."

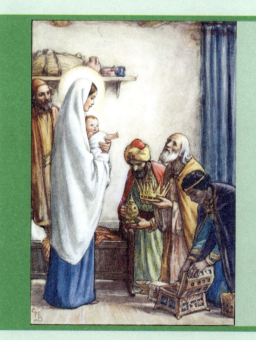

Wise Woman

I was telling my three boys the story of the Nativity and how the Wise Men brought gifts of gold, frankincense, and myrrh for the infant Jesus.

Clearly giving it a lot of thought, my six-year-old observed, "Mom, a Wise Woman would have brought diapers."

He's Moving!

The pastor asks his flock, "What would you like people to say when you're in your casket?"

One parishioner says, "I'd like them to say I worked hard and loved my family."

Another says, "I'd like them to say I helped people."

The third responds, "I'd like them to say, 'Look! I think he's moving!'"

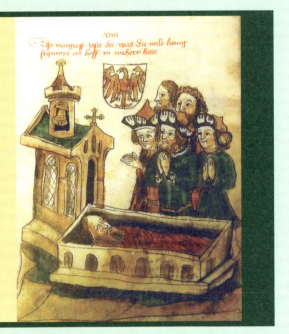

A Prayer to St. Anthony

Teacher: "And when St. Joseph and Our Lady realized they had lost the Holy Child, what do you think was the first thing they did?"

Little Girl: "They knelt down and said a prayer to St. Anthony?"

Hurray for us!

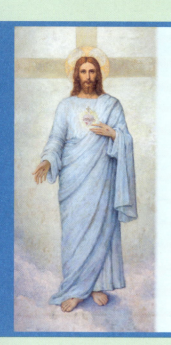

On the way home from First Friday devotions little Johnny asked his mother why after Father said a few words the people said, "Hurray for us."

The mother explained that it was a litany to the Sacred Heart of Jesus and the people were saying, "*Pray* for us."

"It's a Christmas gift from one of our missionaries."

The Flea

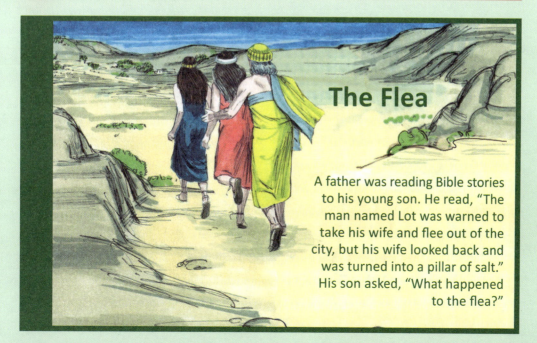

A father was reading Bible stories to his young son. He read, "The man named Lot was warned to take his wife and flee out of the city, but his wife looked back and was turned into a pillar of salt." His son asked, "What happened to the flea?"

"But, Mom, this isn't what I had in mind
when I said I wanted to pump iron!"

Which Service?

One Sunday morning, the pastor noticed little Alex was staring up at the large plaque that hung in the foyer of the church. The plaque was covered with names, and small American flags were mounted on either side of it. The seven-year-old had been staring at the plaque for some time, so the pastor walked up, stood beside the boy, and said quietly, "Good morning Alex."

"Good morning pastor," replied the young man, still focused on the plaque.

"Pastor McGhee, what is this?" Alex asked.

"Well, son, it's a memorial to all the young men and women who died in the service."

Soberly, they stood together, staring at the large plaque. Little Alex's voice was barely audible when he asked, "Which service, the 8:30 or the 11:00?"

The Fatted Calf

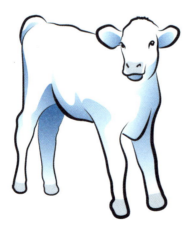

To test the pupils on how well they learned the catechism lesson, the priest asked, "Who was sorry that the Prodigal Son returned?" To which one pupil answered, "The fatted calf!"

Bandaged Children

Some grade school youngsters were asked to write the prayer, "Hail, Holy Queen." One boy wrote, "to you we cry, poor bandaged children of Eve."

More-Tea

A missionary priest in Japan was visiting his parishioners who were scattered around the countryside. At the first house he entered, the kind people prepared a cup of tea for him. Although he disliked tea, he drank it because he knew it would offend them if he refused. It was the same thing at every stop after that: more tea. As the priest thought of the cup of tea awaiting him at every house, he was able to accept it when he thought of it all as mortification (or as he was thinking: more-tea-fication).

Hushers

Six-year-old Angie and her four-year-old brother Joel were sitting together in church. Joel giggled, sang, and talked out loud. Finally, his big sister had enough. "You're not supposed to talk out loud in church."

"Why? Who's going to stop me?" Joel asked.

Angie pointed to the back of the church and said, "See those two men standing by the door? They're hushers."

11

2 |

For creativity to produce good fruit, it has to be guided and trained. Everyone has the ability to be creative, but not everyone's creativity will look the same. Some of us are like potatoes that grow under the soil, having a hidden creativity. Others produce lovely, visible flowers like roses. Some will have insignificant flowers followed by versatile fruits like tomatoes. Let's read a story about two sisters, a long time ago, who creatively used the catch-word "potato" in order to produce the good fruit of virtue.

Potato

"Have you practiced your music today, Nell?" asked Mrs. Layton, as Nell took up a book which she hoped to read undisturbed until supper.

"No, Mamma; but I don't feel like it now," she replied. "This is a lovely story, and I want to finish it."

"I am sorry," said her mother gently, "but tomorrow your music teacher will be here. You had better go to the piano, and practice your lesson several times more."

Nell pouted, and threw aside her book impatiently.

"Oh, dear!" grumbled Nell to Lucy, who was making a dress for their little sister's doll, "isn't this just perfectly horrid! Plaguey old music anyway! I wonder who invented the piano? He ought to have had more sense!"

Nell was fast talking herself into a bad mood. Lucy looked quietly up from her sewing, regarded her sister steadily for a moment, and said, reproachfully: "Nell—potato!"

The word had a magical effect. Nell stopped abruptly, then said in a pleasant tone:

"Why, thank you, Lucy; I forgot." And, cheerily humming a popular tune, she went at once to the piano.

Mrs. Layton, who had overheard the little conversation, paused in astonishment.

"What can be the meaning of this?" she wondered, laughing quietly to herself. "What new game is this? I never knew before that there was so much virtue in a potato. It seems to be an excellent cure for pouting."

She looked toward the library, hesitant to ask for an explanation. From the parlor across the hall came the sound of a faithful running of scales—an evidence that Nell had set to work with a right good will.

"No, I won't spoil their creativity, whatever it is," concluded the lady. "I'll await further developments."

The next Saturday, the children received a visit from Minnie Prescott. Now, Minnie was not a favorite with Lucy and Nell. Mr. Prescott was the owner of the largest bank in the city. Minnie's mother had died several years before, and the child had been spoiled. It was a bright March day, but Minnie did not like the idea of going outside to play.

"Oh!" she cried, "the wind would blow the feathers out of my best hat, and the rough walks ruin my new boots."

The girls tried to entertain her by showing her their books and games.

"They are very nice, but my papa buys me prettier ones," she said. "Let's not look at them any more, but just sit and talk."

So Minnie chatted away, and the others listened while she rattled on, about her fashionable dresses; about the styles, past, present and to come.

At last the young guest pulled out a tiny jeweled watch, glanced at it, and cried, in apparent dismay: "Why, it's five o'clock! Papa will be waiting for me."

Minnie wished her friends good-bye, gave Mrs. Layton a dainty, bird-like kiss, and floated away, saying, "Thank you. I have had a perfectly splendid time. Come and see me soon, girls; and I will show you all my pretty things."

Nell and Lucy watched her leave.

"There she goes!" said Nell.

"Yes, and I'm sure I'm glad," said Lucy, sharply; "She acts so important, and is so proud because she has a watch and a diamond ring. It's only a speck of a diamond, anyway."

"But it is one," replied Nell, who had been rather impressed by the general glitter and flutter about the visitor.

"Minnie is always talking about herself," Lucy went on. "She is just as disagreeable as she can be, with her airs and her showy clothes. I don't see why we can't have more nice dresses than we have. Two for school, and one for Sunday—that's the rule. Mamma says, even if we could afford it, we should not have more than that in a season, as she does not approve of little girls thinking too much of what they wear. She ought to have heard Minnie!"

Lucy was in the midst of another complaint; both were too engrossed to notice that Mrs. Layton had crossed the hall, and stood in the doorway. Just as she was about to speak, Nell laid her hand on her sister's arm and exclaimed, as if upon sudden thought: "Oh—oh—potato!"

To the good lady's amazement, Lucy cut herself short in the middle of a word. After a moment of silence she said, regretfully: "It was unkind of me to talk so about Minnie. She has no mother to tell her what to do, and is not so much to blame if she makes mistakes."

Mrs. Layton turned away. She was puzzled, to say the least. "What possible connection could there be between virtue and potatoes?"

****

"Hurry, Lucy! We'll be late for school," cried Nell one morning, a day or two after the above conversation. Lucy quickly collected her books and joined her sister.

They hastened to the pantry. Nell dragged out the potato basket and tipped out the contents; thereupon, both began picking over the potatoes, each anxious to secure the largest. Then occurred an animated discussion:

"You had the biggest yesterday; it's my turn now," said Lucy, disconsolately, as Nell held aloft a splendid specimen and started hurrying away. "It isn't fair!" continued Lucy; but a timely recollection flashed upon her, and she cried, in a remonstrating tone: "Potato! potato!

Instantly Nell stopped and came slowly back. She looked wistfully at her treasure, then unexpectedly dropped it into Lucy's lap, caught up another of goodly size, dusted it in a trice, and ran off.

The cook, who was busy with her work, paused and held up her hands in wonder. "Wisha! what has come over the childer?" thought she.

Lucy meanwhile, looking a little ashamed, deposited the potato in her school-bag, and prepared to follow, leaving the rest scattered about the floor.

"Indeed, Miss," exclaimed the cook, half in fun, half in earnest, as she surveyed the disorder. "I don't know how it is that ye young ladies can perform such miracles just by crying, 'Potato!' Troth an' it's 'Potato' I'd like to say to yerselves. Look at that dirt on me clane floor! An' whose goin' to tidy up the place, will ye tell me?"

"Oh, excuse me, Bridget!" replied Lucy. "I'll have everything in order in a minute." So saying, she returned, and began picking up the potatoes, and putting them into the basket.

"Och, sure niver mind, Miss!" protested the good-natured cook. "Don't mind, awinna. I'll see to that. It's late for school ye'll be, I'm afeard."

"No, there is really plenty of time," said Lucy, pleasantly; but, having finished her task, she tripped contentedly away.

Bridget watched her out of sight; then she dropped into a chair, and laughed heartily. Mrs. Layton, coming into the kitchen at that moment, looked inquiringly at her.

"Faith, mum," said she, "it's the quarest play that iver was played. You have only to say 'Potato!' to thim, and they become as gintle and obadient as young lambs. But I dunno what it manes at all at all."

"So you have noticed the odd doings too?" said her mistress, smiling.

Thus encouraged, Bridget narrated the episode which had so surprised her.

"Well, this is very remarkable," said Mrs. Layton, as impressed with the story as Bridget could possibly have desired.

That afternoon, she said to her little daughters, when they were all enjoying a cozy chat together: "By the way, won't you let me into your secret? Perhaps your motto may do as much for me, as it has done for you."

"Secret—motto?" asked Lucy, in bewilderment.

"Oh, I know!" exclaimed Nell. "Mamma means 'Potato!'" And she laughed joyously.

"Why, that is no secret," said Lucy. "And we never thought of it as a motto. We are just making a novena of potatoes—that's all."

"A novena of potatoes!" repeated Mrs. Layton, rather surprised.

"Yes," explained Nell, eagerly. "At school we are having a novena for the Feast of the Annunciation. There is a virtue to practice for each day. The first day it was cheerful obedience, the next charity, and so on; today it was consideration for others. Then, as we all wanted to do something for the poor, Mother Superior said that every day, each one who had kept the practice might drop a potato into a barrel; and at the end of the week the barrel would be given to a poor family. Any child who failed, after being reminded once, could not put one in, and nobody was to put in more than one. So we girls call this a novena of potatoes."

"And is the barrel nearly full?" asked Mrs. Layton.

"I should say so!" answered Lucy, with satisfaction. "In that corner of the corridor there are three barrels heaped high with potatoes."

"But what about the motto?" asked Mrs. Layton.

"Lucy and I agreed to help each other to remember the virtue to practice," replied Nell. "If she sees that I am in danger of failing, she says 'Potato!' If I notice that she is forgetting, I cry, 'Potato!' and we both understand."

For the next week Mrs. Layton had a secret of her own. At last, one day when Lucy and Nell came home from school, each was delighted to find in her own room a pretty oil painting of a cluster of beautiful white and purple blossoms.

"Aren't they lovely?" cried Lucy, rapturously.

"How sweet of Mamma to paint them for us!" said Nell, gratefully.

"But what flower is this?" asked Lucy, looking closely at her picture. "It must be something rare. I've never seen it before."

"Look, here is a tiny scroll in the corner," interrupted Nell.

"So there is! Let us spell out the word in the scroll," suggested Lucy.

With eager curiosity they bent over their paintings.

"Why!" exclaimed Lucy, after a moment, beginning to laugh, "it's 'Potato!'"

At the revelation, the two girls broke into a peal of merriment. Mrs. Layton heard their gleeful, ringing voices, and, coming into the room, joined in the mirth.

"But it is not all a jest," said the good mother. "I designed and painted these special pictures so that the flowers might remind you to cultivate, in daily life, the humble virtues which you have begun planting through your 'novena of potatoes.'"

The sportive homily was not forgotten, and, years afterwards, Lucy and Nell would show their children and grandchildren the paintings of the pretty white and purple flowers, and tell the story of "Potato."

Adapted from a story written in 1889 by Mary C. Crowley

Illuminated Bookmark

Just as the girls in the story used "potato help" to remember to practice virtue, you're going to make an illuminated bookmark to help you remember. Color in the illuminated NO design. Underneath, list temptations or faults that you resolve to say "no" to. On the other side of the bookmark, color in the YES design and list the virtues and good deeds that you want to say "yes" to. Cut out your bookmark and use it to remind you of the good habits you want to cultivate. Laminate for durability.

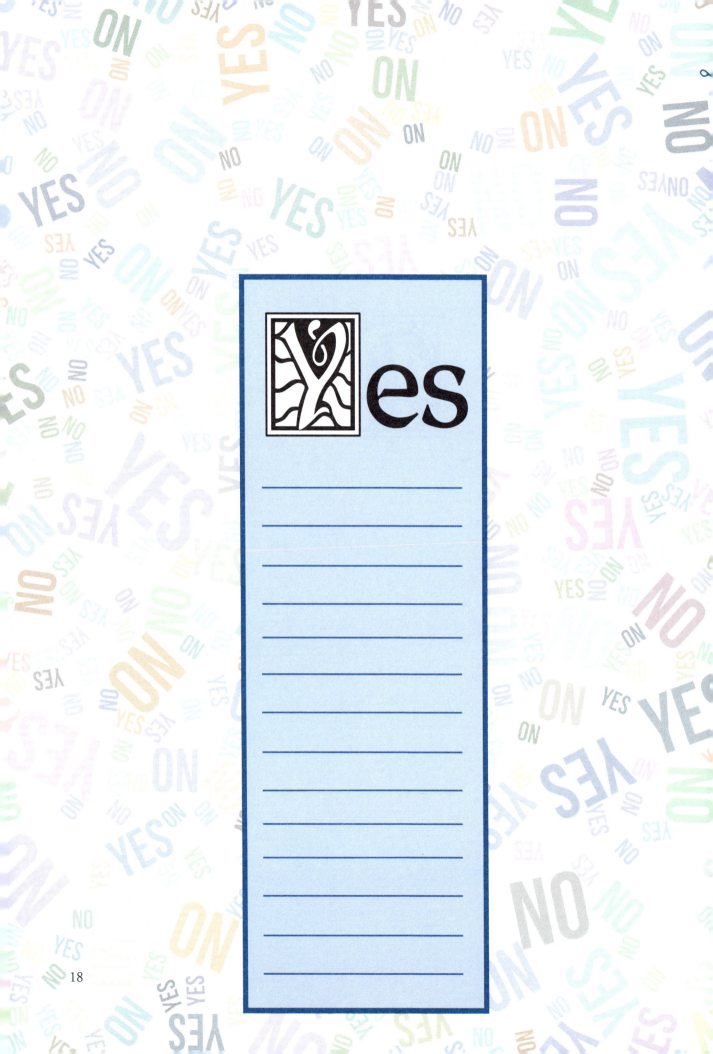

Yes

_____

_____

_____

_____

_____

_____

_____

_____

_____

_____

_____

_____

3

God has been generous to us, giving us many gifts, talents, and abilities. Through creativity, we can share His generosity with others. Don't allow selfishness and vanity to keep you from sharing the gifts that God has given you! Instead, turn to the sacraments for help in strengthening your God-given gifts and learning to use them appropriately. Let's read a story about a vain little window whose misplaced pride keeps it from sharing its gifts with others. Which sacrament does this story remind you of?

The Discontented Mill Window

A tall flour mill once stood in the midst of a busy, noisy town. Its steep, slanting roof was far above any other roof in the place, and its many windows looked out over the chimney tops and into the back yards, and saw all that was going on in them.

Under the very eaves of this slanting roof was a window that was so high above the other windows that from it you could have seen not only all that was being done in the busy city, but the broad, green fields outside of the town, and, on a clear day, you could even have caught a glimpse of the vast ocean which lay shining so mysteriously beyond the end of land. It was because this glimpse of the great ocean could be seen through the little round window that the mill-owner brought many visitors up to the top story to see the beautiful vision. Oftentimes the guests reached the window panting and out of breath from having to climb so many steps, but

they always exclaimed, "How glad I am that I came! How beautiful it is! How beautiful it is!"

Every noon some of the tired, dusty workmen would come and look out of the little round window, sometimes almost forgetting to eat the bread and meat they held in their hands. Oftentimes the window would hear them say, "It rests one's tired bones to know that the great ocean is not so far away after all." There was one pale, sad-faced man who used to come every day and lean his elbows on the window sill and gaze and gaze, as if he were never tired of looking out on the view which the little round window presented.

When the mill whistle sounded its shrill, sharp note, telling the men that the noonday rest was over and that they must be back at their work, the pale, sad-faced man would sigh, and as he turned away, would say softly to himself, "I don't

believe I could stand the grind of this mill life if I didn't get a breath of ocean air from this window each day!"

Once in a while, a good father would bring his children up to the window and, lifting them in his strong arms, would let them see the green fields and shining ocean. Then the children would clap their hands and shout aloud for joy. Occasionally one would beg that he might be allowed to go away from the noisy, dusty town, through the broad, green fields to the endless ocean beyond.

At night when all the town was hushed in sleep, and even the green fields looked cold and dark, and deep shadows seemed to be on every object, the vision of the great ocean was, if possible, more beautiful than during the bright day. At such hours the little round window had the gleam of

the never sleeping waters all to itself, as very few people have courage to climb much in the night, and none of them knew how beautiful the mighty ocean looked in the midst of darkness. So they lost the gleam of the heavenly stars as they were reflected in its wavelets. Sometimes the broad silver path which the moon spread upon the surface of the water looked as if it might be the shining stairway to the heavenly gates themselves, and the little round window felt quite sure that it saw bright angels ascending and descending this silvery stairway just as they had done in the dream of Jacob of old. At such times the little window would tremble all over with delight.

But alas! alas! now comes the sad part of my story. Time passed on, and so many people came to look through the little round window that scarcely a day went by in which the window did not hear exclamations of pleasure and admiration escape from their lips. Soon the foolish little window began to think that the people were talking of it, and not of the vision of the great ocean which could be seen through its round window pane. Thus it grew proud and vain, and thought it somehow must be superior to ordinary glass windows, and therefore it ought not to be treated like them. So when the wet rain clouds came one day, as usual, to wash the dust off the faces of all the windows in the town, the little round window in the top of the tall mill refused to be washed. "Tut, tut, tut!" said the rain, "what nonsense! A window is good for nothing unless it is washed about once in so often."

However, the vain little window would not listen, but held on to the grimy soot and yellow dust which had accumulated upon its surface. Even the rattle of the fierce thunder did not frighten it, and when the wind sighed and sobbed and moaned as if to beg the little window to be sensible and take the washing which the rain was trying to give it, the obstinate window merely shook in its frame and answered, "I tell you I am not like other windows. Everybody admires me. Why should I have to mind that cold, wet rain, just because other windows do? I am not going to give up my soot and my dust. I am going to do just as I please. Am I not above all the other windows? It is well enough for them to be slapped in the face by the rain and even sometimes washed and scrubbed from within, but none of that for me."

And thus the vain, foolish little window lost its chance to be made pure and clean again.

Gradually the dust from the street and the smoke from the neighboring chimneys settled thicker and thicker upon it, and of course the view of the busy, noisy town, of the quiet green fields, and of the great, shining ocean, became dimmer and dimmer until at last they were lost sight of altogether and nothing could be seen but the round form of the window, so thick was the grime and dirt upon it.

Now the men ceased coming to the top story at noon time, and the owner of the mill brought no more guests to its side, and the little round window, left to itself, became sad and lonely. Day after day passed and no one came near it. In fact, people seemed to have forgotten that it was in existence. One day two boys climbed to the attic in which it had been built, and the little round window said eagerly to itself, "Now I shall hear some of the praise that belongs to me." But in a very few moments one of the boys said, "Whew! how close and dark it is up here! Let's go down!" "All right," replied the other, and down they scampered without even so much as noticing the dust-covered window.

At first the window was indignant at what it termed their lack of appreciation. However, as day and night succeeded each other and days grew into weeks, and weeks stretched into a month, the little round window had plenty of time to think, and by and by came the thought, "Why did people ever crowd around me, and climb many stairs to get near me?" Then it recalled the words which it had heard, and with the recalling came the realization that the talk had all been about the beautiful view which it presented, and not about itself.

Then, indeed, it would have hung its head in shame if it could have done so, but although a window has a face, it has no head, you know, so that all it could do was to turn itself on its wooden pivots until its round face was ready to catch any drop of rain that might fall. Nor did it have long to wait. The beautiful white clouds which had been drifting dreamily across the blue sky changed into soft gray, and then their under parts became a heavy, dark gray, and soon they began massing themselves together. The wind arose and hurried the smaller clouds across the

sky as a general might marshal his troops for a battle, and in a little while the whole heavens were covered with gray, not even a single spot of blue sky remained, nor could one yellow sunbeam be seen on the whole landscape. The low rumble of thunder could now be heard, and quick flashes of lightning darted from raincloud to raincloud and back again as if they were messengers sent to see if all was in readiness for the storm. Soon down poured the rain.

Not even the thirsty earth itself was more glad to receive the tens of thousands of water drops than was the little round window in the top story of the tall mill. It not only had its outside face freed from the dust and soot, but with some help from the wind, it managed to turn its inside face out and thus be cleansed within as well as without.

At last the storm passed away; the sun shone again; the trees rustled their fresh, shining, green leaves, and all nature rejoiced in the renewed life which the reviving rain had brought with it. The little window fairly glistened as its shining face caught the golden radiance of the last beams of the setting sun. "Ah, look at the little mill window!" said the miller's wife, "the rain has washed it bright and clean. See how it reflects the sunset. Tomorrow we will go up and get a view of the ocean from it—I had almost forgotten how beautiful it was."

Adapted from a story written in 1895 by
Elizabeth Harrison

Listening and Looking

Listening and looking are important ways to be charitable. They indicate a high level of mature creativity. They are the foundation of building and strengthening loving relationships with God and others. An old Latin saying translates into the idea that there is nothing in the mind that has not first come through our senses. By engaging our senses of sight and hearing with care, we strengthen our thoughtful responses to each other.

The next time you have an argument or disagreement with someone else, try the following. Stop whatever you are doing, look at each other, and focus on the other person's viewpoint.

Only one person has to do this, and the disagreement will become easier to resolve. Solutions will appear because you are taking the time to express your love creatively. In other words, you are taking the time to attend to God's will, which is that we love one another. It sounds very simple to stop and listen and look at another person, but if you are not in the habit of listening carefully, you will have to force yourself to do so. If you have a particular unresolved situation, come to your senses! Take the time to respond creatively.

Over the next few days, complete the following activities to develop your "listening and looking" skills.

☐ Ask a parent to sit down with you and state what he believes are three of your opinions on various subjects as you sit quietly and listen without interrupting. Then state what you think your parent's opinions on those same subjects are while your parent listens. Possible subjects—favorite food, music, color, friend; a difficult academic subject; a hobby; a possible vocation; greatest talent. Take turns. This is a good exercise in listening and in not interrupting. It can be difficult not to correct someone who is talking about your personal opinions. Why in the world would he think that you like artichokes and the color orange?!

☐ Listen to someone talking on the radio or on television. Don't listen to the meaning of the words. Listen for the emotions behind the words. A good listener will pay attention to the speaker's feelings. Is the person sad, happy, frightened, awed, embarrassed?

☐ Take turns with your mom or dad or sibling saying each other's name aloud. Say it softly, loudly, in a whisper, in a sing-song. Which way do you each like best to hear your name spoken?

☐ Stand face to face with a family member and take turns following each other's moves as if you are mirroring each other. These can be as subtle as a raised eyebrow or as obvious as a belly laugh.

☐ Listen to music and draw the rhythm with a pencil. Does it jump, dive, stop, rise, slide, leap, cascade?

4

Lack of appreciation of what God has created—in nature, in the people around us, and in ourselves—stifles our creativity. God cared enough to create an awesome, beautiful world for us. In this story, Tommy is shown how to appreciate the well-planned, creative, and beautiful world exactly the way God made it.

The Colored Lands

Once upon a time there was a 10-year-old boy whose name was Tommy. Tommy was sitting one very hot afternoon on a green lawn outside the cottage that his father and mother had rented in the country. The cottage had a bare white-washed wall; and at that moment it seemed to Tommy very bare. The summer sky was of a blank blue, which at that moment seemed to him very blank. The dull yellow thatch looked very dull and rather dusty; and the row of flower-pots in front of him, with red flowers in them, looked irritatingly straight, so that he wanted to knock some of them over like ninepins. Even the grass around him moved him only to pluck it up in a vicious way; almost as if he were wicked enough to wish it was his sister's hair. Only he had no sister; and indeed no brothers. He was an only child and at that moment rather a lonely child, which is not necessarily the same thing.

He continued to pull out the grass like the green hair of an imaginary and irritating sister, when he was surprised to hear a stir and a step behind him, on the side of the garden far away from the garden gate.

He saw walking toward him a rather strange-looking young man wearing blue spectacles. He was clad in a suit of such very light gray that it looked almost white in the strong sunlight; and he had long loose hair of such very light or faint yellow that the hair might almost have been white as well as the clothes. He had a large limp straw hat to shade him from the sun; and, presumably for the same purpose, he flourished in his left hand a Japanese parasol of a bright peacock green. Tommy had no idea how he had come onto that side of the garden; but it appeared most probable that he had jumped over the hedge.

All that he said was, with the most casual and familiar accent, "Got the blues?"

Tommy did not answer and perhaps did not understand; but the strange young man proceeded with great composure to take off his blue spectacles.

"Blue spectacles are a strange cure for the blues," he said cheerfully. "Just look through these for a minute."

Tommy was moved to a mild curiosity and peered through the glasses; there certainly was something weird and quaint about the discoloration of everything; the red roses black and the white wall blue, and the grass a bluish green like the plumes of a peacock.

"Looks like a new world, doesn't it?" said the stranger. "Wouldn't you like to go wandering in a blue world once in a blue moon?"

"Yes," said Tommy and put the spectacles down with a rather puzzled air. Then his expression changed to surprise; for the extraordinary young man had put on another pair of spectacles, and this time they were red.

"Try these," he said affably. "These, I suppose, are revolutionary glasses. Some people call it looking through rose-colored spectacles. Others call it seeing red."

Tommy tried the spectacles, and was quite startled by the effect; it looked as if the whole world were on fire. The sky was of a glowing or rather glaring purple, and the roses were not so much red as red-hot. He took off the glasses almost in alarm, only to note that the young man's immovable countenance was now adorned with yellow spectacles. By the time that these had been followed by green spectacles, Tommy thought he had been looking at four totally different landscapes.

"And so," said the young man, "you would like to travel in a country of your favorite color. I did it once myself."

Tommy was staring up at him with round eyes.

"Who are you?" he asked suddenly.

"I'm not sure," replied the other. "I rather think I am your long-lost brother."

"But I haven't got a brother," objected Tommy.

"It only shows how very long-lost I was," replied his remarkable relative. "But I assure you that, before they managed to long-lose me, I used to live in this house myself."

"When you were a boy like me?" asked Tommy with some reviving interest.

"Yes," said the stranger gravely. "When I was a boy and very like you. I also used to sit on the grass and wonder what to do with myself. I also got tired of the blank white wall. I also got tired even of the beautiful blue sky. I also thought the thatch was just thatch and wished the roses did not stand in a row."

"Why, how do you know I felt like that?" asked the boy, who was rather frightened.

"Why, because I felt like that myself," said the other with a smile.

Then after a pause he went on.

"And I also thought that everything might look different if the colors were different; if I could wander about on blue roads between blue fields and go on wandering till all was blue. And a Wizard who was a friend of mine actually granted my wish, and I found myself walking in forests of great blue flowers like gigantic lupins and larkspurs, with only glimpses now and then of pale blue skies over a dark blue sea. The trees were inhabited by blue jays and bright blue kingfishers. Unfortunately they were also inhabited by blue baboons."

"Were there any people in that country?" inquired Tommy. The traveler paused to reflect for a moment; then he nodded and said:

"Yes; but of course wherever there are people, there are troubles. You couldn't expect all the people in the Blue Country to get on with each other very well.

"Blue-books are the only kind of book allowed there. That is why I decided to leave. With the assistance of my friend the Wizard I obtained a passport to cross the frontier, which was a very vague and shadowy one, like the fine shade between two tints of the rainbow. I only felt that I was passing over peacock-colored seas and meadows and the world was growing greener and greener till I knew I was in a Green Country. You would think that was more restful, and so it was, up to a point. The point was when I met the celebrated Green Man. And then there is always a certain amount of limitation in the work and trade of these beautiful harmonious landscapes. Have you ever lived in a country where all the people were green-grocers? I think not. After all, I asked myself, why should all grocers be green? I felt myself longing to look at a yellow grocer. I saw rise up before me the glowing image of a red grocer. It was just about this time that I floated insensibly into the Yellow Country; but I did not stay there very long. At first it was very splendid; a radiant scene of sunflowers and golden crowns; but I soon found it was almost entirely filled with Yellow Fever. So I faded through an orange haze until I came to the Red Country, and it was there that I really found out the truth of the matter."

"What did you find out?" asked Tommy, who was beginning to listen much more attentively.

"Well, do you know," said the young man, "it is a curious fact that in a rose-red city you cannot really see any roses. Everything is a great deal too red. Your eyes are tired until it might just as well all be brown. After I had been walking for ten minutes on scarlet grass under a scarlet sky and scarlet trees, I called out in a loud voice, 'Oh, this is all a mistake.' And the moment I had said that the whole red vision vanished; and I found myself standing in quite a different sort of place; and opposite me was my old friend the Wizard, whose face and long rolling beard were all one sort of colorless color like ivory, but his eyes of a colorless blinding brilliance like diamonds.

"'Well,' he said, 'you don't seem very easy to please. If you can't put up with any of these countries, or any of these colors, you shall jolly well make a country of your own.'

"And then I looked round me at the place to which he had brought me; and a very curious place it was. It lay in great ranges of mountains, in layers of different colors; and it looked something like sunset clouds turned solid and something like those maps that mark geological soils, grown gigantic. But the most curious thing of all was that right in front of me there was a huge chasm in the hills that opened into sheer blank daylight. The curious thing about it was that if you splashed some of the colored earths upon it, they remained where you had thrown them, as a bird hangs in the air. And there the Wizard told me, rather impatiently, to make what sort of world I

liked for myself, for he was sick of my grumbling at everything.

"So I set to work very carefully; first blocking in a great deal of blue, because I thought it would throw up a sort of square of white in the middle; and then I thought a fringe of a sort of dead gold would look well along the top of the white; and I spilt some green at the bottom of it. As for red, I had already found out the secret about red. You have to have a very little of it to make a lot of it. So I just made a row of little blobs of bright red on the white just above the green; and as I went on working at the details, I slowly discovered what I was doing; which is what very few people ever discover in this world. I found I had put back, bit by bit, the whole of that picture over there in front of us. I had made that white cottage with the thatch and that summer sky behind it and that green lawn below; and the row of the red flowers just as you see them now. That is how they come to be there. I thought you might be interested to know it."

And with that he turned so sharply that Tommy had not time to turn and see him jump over the hedge; for Tommy remained staring at the cottage, with a new look in his eyes.

Adapted from a story by G.K. Chesterton

Beautiful World

Often we look, but do not see or hear. Take the time to look and listen actively with your soul and your body to God's creation. Over the next few days, complete the following activities to develop your "listening and looking" skills.

☐ Take a handful of sand or dirt. How many colors are you holding? How does it feel? What does it smell like?

☐ Look closely at a flower, but don't pull it apart. Don't disconnect it. Instead, see how the stem joins the petals, how the petals overlap.

☐ Record your voice. Listen to it. Does it sound strange to you?

☐ If you have a pet, name all the colors on the pet. Goldfish aren't just gold-colored. Rabbits aren't just brown and gray.

☐ Go to a nearby park or other wide-open space and watch the sky as the sun sets or rises. Huddle together if it's cold. Watch God paint the clouds.

☐ Run your hands over different familiar objects in your house. How does your own bedroom wall feel? Your bed covers? Your floor? Your favorite book? Your winter coat?

☐ What senses do you use during the Holy Mass? Do you have incense and beeswax candles? What about the holy water? Are the pews cushioned or hard? Are there beautiful flowers or banners? Do you hear any bells?

5

We are bodies with minds and souls. We are a little trinity that is always in danger of losing its perspective. Decisions about life require that we know what is most important to us. Read the following short stories that highlight how unique each person's perspective is. Keeping a balance between extreme perspectives is a good thing to practice.

The Father & the Son

One day, a father of a very wealthy family took his son on a trip to the country with the firm purpose of showing his son how poor people live. They spent a couple of days and nights on the farm of what would be considered a very poor family. On their return from their trip, the father asked his son, "How was the trip?"

"It was great, Dad."

"Did you see how poor people live?" the father asked.

"Oh yeah," said the son.

"So, tell me, what did you learn from the trip?" asked the father.

The son answered, "I saw that we have one dog and they had four. We have a pool that reaches to the middle of our garden, and they have a creek that has no end. We have imported lanterns in our garden, and they have the stars at night. Our patio reaches to the front yard, and they have the whole horizon. We have a small piece of land to live on, and they have fields that go beyond our sight. We have servants who serve us, but they serve others. We buy our food, but they grow theirs. We have walls around our property to protect us; they have friends to protect them."

The boy's father was speechless.

Then his son added, "Thanks, Dad, for showing me how poor we are."

The Philosopher & the Boatman

A philosopher, who wished to cross a turbulent stream of water, engaged a boatman to row him over. While on the way, he asked the boatman if he understood algebra.

"Algebra!" exclaimed the boatman, "I never heard of it before. I know nothing about it."

"Then," said the philosopher, "one quarter of your life is lost. But perhaps you know something about metaphysics?"

"Met-a, met-a what?" asked the boatman. "Oh, you wish to know if I ever studied physics. Not much, sir; I have no taste for such things."

"You don't understand me," said the philosopher. "I wished to know whether you have any knowledge of metaphysics—the science which explains the principles and causes of all things existing—philosophy."

"I never heard that word before," replied the boatman. "My father was a ferryman, and I have followed the same business ever since I was strong enough to row a boat. I know nothing of Met-a—what do you call it?"

"Well, if you know nothing of metaphysics, then you have lost another quarter of your life. But perhaps you know something about astronomy?" asked the philosopher.

"I know nothing about those things," said the boatman. "I have had other business to attend to."

"Then I must inform you that another quarter of your life is lost. But what is the matter with this boat, and why are you taking off your coat?" asked the philosopher.

"Don't you see," said the boatman, "that the boat has sprung a leak, and is fast sinking? Can you swim?"

"Swim? No, indeed! You don't expect a philosopher like me to swim, do you?"

"Then," said the boatman, "if you cannot swim the whole of your life is lost, for the boat is rapidly sinking, and will soon go to the bottom."

"Ah me!" exclaimed the philosopher, "how willingly would I part with all my other knowledge, if by so doing, I could acquire the art of swimming!"

Adapted from a story written in 1875, author unknown

Recipe for Happiness

What is your perspective about what makes a person happy? Today you're going to be creative and write your own recipe for happiness. Using one of the templates on the next page, think of those things that truly make you happy and write them down in a recipe format. When finished, laminate and place your recipe card in your prayer book or post it in a spot that will remind you of what is truly important in life. Read the sample recipes below to get you started.

Recipe for Happiness

Take a little dash of water,
and a little leaven of prayer,
And a little bit of morning gold,
dissolved in the morning air;
Add to your meal some merriment,
and a thought for kith and kin,
And then, as a prime ingredient,
a plenty of work thrown in,
But spice it all with the essence of
love and a little whiff of play;
Let the wise old Book, and a glance
above, complete the well-made day.

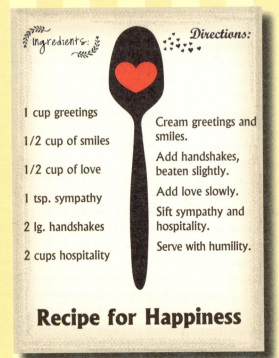

Ingredients:

1 cup greetings

1/2 cup of smiles

1/2 cup of love

1 tsp. sympathy

2 lg. handshakes

2 cups hospitality

Directions:

Cream greetings and smiles.

Add handshakes, beaten slightly.

Add love slowly.

Sift sympathy and hospitality.

Serve with humility.

Recipe for Happiness

Ingredients:

Directions:

J.O.Y. is a recipe for happiness!

Jesus First

Others Second

Yourself Last

J.O.Y. is a recipe for happiness!

Jesus First

Others Second

Yourself Last

6 God doesn't want us all to be artists or musicians, but He does want us each to discover how we can know, love, and serve Him best. For each person, that knowledge, love, and service will be unique. In this story, Philip uses the gift of his beautiful voice to help others experience the birth of Christ in a deeper way. Notice that he doesn't fully understand why his song moves his audience to tears; he doesn't realize the great gift he has given the people who are listening. It is the same way with the gifts and talents God has given us. Often we don't realize just how much it means to people when we share our creativity with love.

His First Appearance

Philip stepped out from behind the scenes and advanced to the middle of the stage.

At sight of the boy with the young face there was a succession of "ohs" and "ahs" from the balcony down to the orchestra circle.

"The brave darling!" came from a lady in tones clearer than she intended; and then the greatest applause of the evening awoke the echoes of the magnificent building.

With his hands behind his back, his head erect, Philip glanced smilingly about the theater. To him they were all friends. And in answer to that smile, there was scarce one in the audience who did not return it, with nods and bows and eyes that told of friendship and good will.

At the first sound of the piano, a silence suddenly fell upon that great assemblage. The prelude was played, the critical moment had come; and Philip, with the skilled manner of one who loved to sing, slipped easily and sweetly into the melody.

His opening notes, full and true, though not very loud, sent a thrill through every listener. At first it was only the voice, so free, so sweet, which charmed each listening ear. But presently it was something far above and beyond the reach of musical sound. For almost at once his face took on an expression which told the audience that with this little soprano, music and feeling were moving hand in hand. While his tongue syllabled the holy night, his soul saw it—saw the stars, saw the earth waking from its slumber of sin and of death.

For Philip there was no audience. The things that were had become as the things that are not, and, at one bound, his imagination had leaped across the centuries and gained the fields that lay still and breathless in the solemn midnight of the olden days.

For Philip instead of an audience there was a vision. A great light shone down upon the plains, a multitude of the heavenly host bathed and floated in its splendor, and the shepherds were either face downward upon the ground, or holding their arms before their eyes lest the splendor of God should strike them dead.

The song had become more than a song. It had risen to a drama—and its subject was the Redemption.

When Philip came to the line,—

"A thrill of hope, the weary world rejoices,"

his voice sank so low that many held their breath lest they should lose the least bit of the lovely sounds. On the word "thrill" his voice so quivered that not only the sound, but the thing signified passed from heart to heart like echoes among the answering hills.

"Fall on your knees!"

All the fullness, all the vibrant power of that extraordinary voice, went into these words. One might fancy that the singer was an inspired and majestic messenger from on high, calling upon all to adore.

"Oh, hear the angel voices!"

With the ending of this phrase his voice died away; there was a pause while Philip, and the audience, seemed to listen for the strains which once made the night of nights resound with "Glory be to God on high, and on earth peace to men of good will."

While Philip thus paused, the piano was silent: the piano was silent, and the listeners were silent. It was as though each one held his breath, and was waiting in tense expectation to catch the accents of the heavenly choirs.

Then suddenly, with triumph and joy in every tone, with an echo of the gladness born of the gladdest tidings that ever fell upon mortal ear, with inspiration born of perfect faith, he trebled forth in a volume of loveliness:—

"Noel! Noel! O night when Christ was born!
Noel! Noel! O night, O night divine!"

The first stanza was finished, and Philip, who was not an angel, despite his voice, and very much of a boy, glanced cheerfully upon the audience, which, though he knew it not, he had bewitched.

A moment before he had been on the plains of Bethlehem, he had brought his audience with him, and left them there with the angels; but he, he himself, bounded in an instant from the first to the nineteenth century and was back in Milwaukee and in the Pabst Theater looking about at the sea of faces, and wondering why so many people were wiping their eyes with their handkerchiefs.

The pianist launched Philip into the second stanza. The sweetness, the pathos, were still with him; but the inspiration of the first stanza was lacking. Philip remained unconscious of the sights and sounds around him; yet though he led not the way, he succeeded in keeping his hearers whither he had already brought them on the wings of sound.

However, as he went on in this second stanza, the music and the words gradually drew his thoughts and feelings back to the hills where the shepherds kept watch. His eyes lost sight of what was before them and looked into the far East and the far times when night was truly made divine. Again the inspiration returned, again his voice rang out with all the spirit of angelic joy. The effect upon the audience was more striking than before, and while they sat thus enraptured, Philip bowed and left the stage.

Adapted from a story written in 1904 by Rev. Francis Finn

Bethlehem Bread

You know that Jesus is the Bread of Life, but did you also know that Bethlehem means "House of Bread"? To honor Him, and His "House of Bread," make this very easy, inexpensive, no-knead treat. Share it with your family!

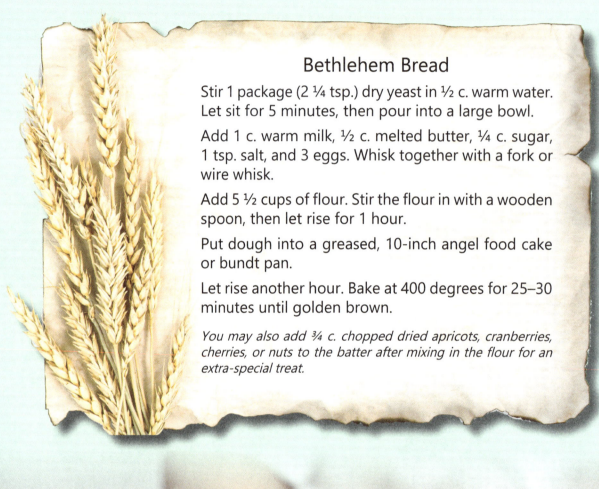

Bethlehem Bread

Stir 1 package (2 ¼ tsp.) dry yeast in ½ c. warm water. Let sit for 5 minutes, then pour into a large bowl.

Add 1 c. warm milk, ½ c. melted butter, ¼ c. sugar, 1 tsp. salt, and 3 eggs. Whisk together with a fork or wire whisk.

Add 5 ½ cups of flour. Stir the flour in with a wooden spoon, then let rise for 1 hour.

Put dough into a greased, 10-inch angel food cake or bundt pan.

Let rise another hour. Bake at 400 degrees for 25–30 minutes until golden brown.

You may also add ¾ c. chopped dried apricots, cranberries, cherries, or nuts to the batter after mixing in the flour for an extra-special treat.

7

Silence of mind and body are often lacking in our lives, but they are necessary for developing true creativity. God doesn't want us to be too busy to listen to Him. Prayer is the most fundamental method of reflection. It slows us down and helps us put first things first. Let's read about a young shepherd who was not too busy to notice Mary and Joseph, and who was later rewarded for his attentiveness.

Aser the Shepherd

My father was a shepherd, the guardian of the Temple flocks destined for sacrifice, and the sacred character of his charge and the solemn destiny of the little lambs I loved early mingled with my childish impressions, and made me a grave and thoughtful child.

There was a prediction that the Messias would be revealed from "the tower of the flock," on the outskirts of Bethlehem. This of course I, a child of five, did not know; but I have since heard it, and how in the longing and degradation of Israel she thirsted and daily prayed with renewed fervor for the coming of Him who was to deliver her.

When I was but five came the enrolling of the entire province under Cyrinus, and the people thronged the highways; and I, a serious, big-eyed little shepherd, tended my own pet lamb all day lovingly, and watched the crowds pass by.

It was late in the afternoon, toward night, a still and peaceful day in December. Two travelers came down the road, a man leading a donkey upon which was seated a woman. The man's face was grave and careworn, earnest, kindly, even reverent in expression; the woman's face was veiled, and her air was very youthful.

As they passed me, nursing my beloved little lamb and looking at them with the solemn gaze of early childhood, the man glanced at me with a half smile, and the young girl's beautiful eyes smiled too at me over the white linen folded to their lids. Something in the look she gave me drew me out of my usual timid reticence.

I sprang to my feet and bowed almost to the grass. "Hail, beautiful lady," I said, "and a safe journey to thee."

The eyes beamed back at me, she murmured a blessing and thanks to me, while her guardian smiled down on me gently, and thanked me for my good wish, amused, as I now see, at the contrast between my gravity and my stature.

They passed on; but I had lost interest in whatever or whoever might come after them, and carrying my lamb, I went back from the roadside to find my father.

My mother died when I was born, and my father filled the place of both parents to me as far as lay in his power. I was his constant companion, and it was not unusual for me to sleep out of doors, except during the rainy season, while he watched his flocks.

On the night of the afternoon when I had saluted the heavenly eyed young traveler I was to follow my custom, for though it was December the air was not sharp, and I was used to exposure.

I was in the depths of the most profound slumber when I was half aroused by the stirring of my pet lamb, and opened my sleepy eyes to a light that blinded me and made me close them again hastily.

The air was full of sweet music, but nothing ever seems particularly amazing to a young child, probably because the whole world is new and strange to him, and I was one whose lonely life made my mind full of such fancies that these sounds were to me only part of my dreams.

I should very likely have fallen asleep again had not my father called me in such hushed and awestruck tones that it frightened me and waked me thoroughly. "Aser, Aser, come thou also to witness. Bring me the boy."

No one could have stirred to obey him, nor was it necessary. Trembling I stood at his side, shading my eyes, and kneeling beside him, trying to gaze upward in the blinding beauty of the light around me, wondering what and whence was the immense multitude of radiant, glorious beings, singing in such strains as the little shepherd boy could never describe, nor as I now know could any one, however old and wise, for the tongue of man has no words for the song of angels.

How long I looked and listened I knew not. At last the heavenly chant ceased, the dazzling light, the beings of resplendent beauty disappeared, and we were alone again on Bethlehem's plain, with only the stars that David had called upon to praise the Lord watching over the city of the king. The dogs, which had been crouching in terror, stirred and crept to the shepherds, each thrusting his nose into his master's hand for explanation of the mystery. The familiar, homely contact of his dog's head aroused my father, and he gasped, catching his breath in a sob of profound emotion:—

"Come, let us adore Him," he said, rising; and I saw in the starlight that he was pale, and the tears streamed down his cheeks.

"Who, Father? Is Jehovah come into the bush again?" I asked.

"He for whom we wait has come," replied my father, solemnly. "The Deliverer, the Messias is born in David's city, as it is written, and it is revealed to us; this is the watch tower of prophecy, and we are chosen to spread the tidings. Hear, O Israel, the Lord thy God, the Lord is one, and thou art remembered of Him. 'Praise the Lord, for He is good; for His mercy endureth forever. Give glory to the God of Heaven; for His mercy endureth forever.'"

Swinging me up on his shoulder he set forth, followed by his men, all chanting the glorious canticle of him to whose line of old the Messias was promised. And thus chanting, unmolested in the silent hours after midnight, we reached the stable in Bethlehem, where a light showed dimly through the open door, and here we paused.

My father set me down, and drawing a mantle from his shoulders, laid it over my head, saying, "Cover thy head, Aser, for the place is holy." Taking my hand, he led me silently in.

I did not know what we had come to see; but my eyes rested on the grave man whom I had seen that afternoon. I quickly looked further, and saw, not far from where I stood, the young girl who had been with him.

She half lay on her right side on the straw, but she leaned on her elbow in such a way that her attitude was rather like kneeling than reclining. Her beautiful eyes were fastened on a tiny baby by her side, wrapped in swaddling-bands, and she saw not us nor anyone except the Infant.

Child as I was, I was awed by the look of adoration and love on her face, a look which I was then too young to understand, though now I can imagine the thoughts that must have filled the mind of the maiden Mary, who was also the mother of that Child for whom prophets had prayed and Israel waited.

My father knelt involuntarily, and all his men did likewise.

The man came forward and greeted us kindly. "How did you learn of this?" he asked.

"The angels came as we watched our flocks, and they told us a Savior was born in the city of David," my father answered simply. "We are shepherds of the Temple flocks, and to us was revealed the birth, as it is foretold,

that the announcement of His coming should be from the tower of the flock."

"God is great," answered the man, solemnly. The young mother had been listening, aroused to attention by my father's words. "Come, first chosen of God's chosen people," she said.

Her voice thrilled me as her gaze had done. I snatched my hand from my father's and ran to her side. Her face grew even brighter with joy than its shining happiness of a few moments before.

"The nearest to Heaven should be first," she murmured, and held her Babe for me to see.

What I knew, what I understood of the great mystery before me, it is impossible to imagine now. My little soul was filled with awe, and yet my small being thrilled with love for the helpless Babe and that wonderful maiden.

The men arose and crept slowly forward. Mary rose to her feet and held the Babe on high. "Behold Him," she said, and they fell backward and kissed the hem of her mantle, and then timidly pressed the Infant's tiny foot to their lips.

"But thou, my little one, lay thy kiss here," and she held out the little frail right hand of the Child.

I kissed the soft palm just where, later, it touched the head of my own baby in blessing, and where, later still, I saw the gaping nail wound.

My father raised me once more to his shoulder, and we set forth back again from the stable cave. Simple shepherds as they were, my father and his men understood the great event which in the mysterious providence of God had been revealed to them first of all Israel.

Early in the morning, taking me with him, and leaving his flocks in charge of his underlings, my father went about spreading the tidings of the wonders of the night, so that by sunset it was known even in Jerusalem that the angels had revealed to the shepherds on Bethlehem's plains the fulfillment of the hope of Israel.

Adapted from a story written in 1904 by Marion Taggart

Praying with the Psalms

In the story you just read, Aser's father quoted from Scripture. You, too, are familiar with Scripture; you hear the Word of God each Sunday at Mass. This week you're going to begin compiling a Book of Psalms that you can use to memorize Scripture like Aser's father did. Read over the psalms provided on pages 43–44. Choose your favorites. (You can also choose psalms from your own Bible.) Now write out the psalms you chose on the decorated psalm pages that follow. Start memorizing the psalms. An easy way to begin is to include them in your daily prayers. Soon you'll have them memorized! When you have successfully memorized a psalm, color the angel on the psalm page using colored pencils. When all your psalms are memorized and colored, remove the pages from the book and fold and staple. Now color the cover of your Book of Psalms!

Psalm 138:3
When I called, You answered me;
You built up strength within me.

Psalm 18:2–3
I love you, Lord, my strength,
my rock, my fortress, my savior.

Psalm 139:13–14
You formed my inmost being;
You knit me in my mother's womb.
I praise You, because I am wonderfully made;
wonderful are Your works!

Psalm 27:1
The Lord is my light and my salvation;
whom should I fear?
The Lord is my life's refuge;
of whom should I be afraid?

Psalm 119:111–112
Your will is my heritage for ever,
the joy of my heart.
I set myself to carry out Your will
in fullness, for ever.

Psalm 96:1–2
O sing to the Lord a new song;
sing to the Lord, all the earth!
Sing to the Lord, bless His name;
tell of His salvation from day to day.

Psalm 143:8
In the morning let me know Your love
for I put my trust in You.
Make me know the way I should walk:
to You I lift up my soul.

Psalm 104:33–34
I will sing to the Lord as long as I live;
I will sing praise to my God while I have being.
May my thoughts be pleasing to Him,
for I rejoice in the Lord.

Psalm 25:4–5
Make known to me Your ways, Lord;
teach me Your paths.
Guide me by Your fidelity and teach me,
for You are God my savior,
for You I wait all the day long.

Psalm 95:6–7
O come, let us worship and bow down,
let us kneel before the Lord, our Maker!
For He is our God,
and we are the people of His pasture,
and the sheep of His hand.

Psalm 27:4
One thing I ask of the Lord; this I seek:
To dwell in the Lord's house
all the days of my life,
To gaze on the Lord's beauty,
to behold His temple.

Psalm 121:1–2
I raise my eyes toward the mountains.
From whence shall come my help?
My help comes from the Lord,
the maker of heaven and earth.

Psalm 91:11
For He commands His angels with regard to
you, to guard you wherever you go.

Psalm 103:19–20
The Lord has established His throne in the
heavens, and his kingdom rules over all.
Bless the Lord, O you His angels,
you mighty ones who do His word,
hearkening to the voice of His word!

Psalm 27:13–14
I believe I shall see the Lord's goodness
in the land of the living.
Wait for the Lord, take courage;
be stouthearted, wait for the Lord!

Psalm 46:10–11
Be still, and know that I am God.
I am exalted among the nations,
I am exalted in the earth!
The Lord of hosts is with us;
the God of Jacob is our refuge.

Psalm 19:14
Let the words of my mouth and the
meditation of my heart
be acceptable in Thy sight,
O Lord, my rock and my redeemer.

Psalm 23:2–3
The Lord is my shepherd;
there is nothing I lack.
In green pastures He has me lie down;
to still waters He leads me;
He restores my soul.

Book of Psalms

I will give thanks to the Lord

with my whole heart;

I will tell of all Your wonders.

I will rejoice in You and be glad,

and sing psalms to Your name,

O Most High. (Psalm 9:2–3)

LET EVERYTHING THAT
HATH BREATH
PRAISE THE LORD.

8 Sometimes we think about creativity as something that doesn't require thought or effort. But acting without thinking, being haphazard, sloppy, or lazy, is not truly creative. Creativity demands decisions and a reasonable evaluation of those decisions. Let's read about a saint who made thoughtful and loving decisions and found creative ways to care for those who were uncared for.

Friend of Children

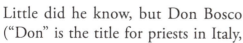

by Elaine Woodfield

It was Our Lady's special feast day, and Fr. John Bosco hurried to the church of St. Francis of Assisi in Turin, Italy, in the early hours of the morning. He didn't want to be late. He had a special love for Our Lady, and was very grateful for her love and prayers. Why? Because that very year, 1841, he, John Bosco, had been ordained a priest. A priest! When he heard the bishop say to him, "You are a priest forever," Fr. Bosco felt as if he were the most happy man in the world. Our Lady's help and prayers had made his dream of becoming a priest come true. Today was the feast of her Immaculate Conception, and today Fr. John Bosco would say Mass in her honor to thank her.

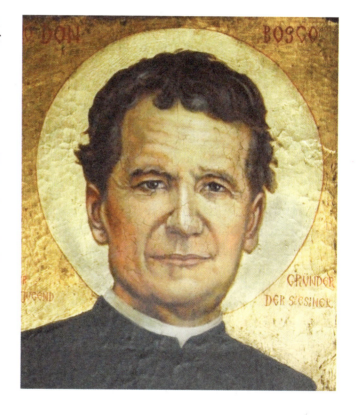

Little did he know, but Don Bosco ("Don" is the title for priests in Italy, like "Father" is here) was about to meet someone who would change his life, and the lives of countless children, men, and women, forever. Who was this person?

He was a ragged, dirty boy named Bartholomew. Because of him, thousands and thousands of boys and girls were saved from lives of crime, poverty, dirt, and hatred. Countless people who would never have known God or His love for them were taught the Faith. From this Faith grew countless prayers, acts of kindness and heroism, and acts of adoration of God who is so merciful.

But I'm getting ahead of the story.

Don Bosco entered the church and hurried to the sacristy, which is the room in which priests prepare for Mass. There he vested, or put on his priestly clothing to say Mass, while saying special prayers. All of a sudden he heard a noise.

A tall boy with snarled hair and a dirty face ran into the room, followed by the church janitor, who was chasing him.

"If you can't serve Mass, then get out!" shouted the janitor as he hit the boy.

"Stop that at once!" said Don Bosco. "Why are you doing this?"

"You don't know how to serve Mass! What are you doing here? Leave at once!" the janitor shouted at the boy. Then he turned to Don Bosco. "Father, I let him in because I thought he was sent to replace your altar boy. But he doesn't want to serve your Mass!"

"Do you have a reason?" asked kindly Don Bosco.

"I don't know how," said the boy. "I just wanted to see what it looks like back here. Besides, it's warm in here." The boy looked cold. Don Bosco wondered if the boy lived on the street.

The janitor was about to throw the boy out the door when Don Bosco held up his hand.

"Let him stay," he said, putting a friendly arm around the boy's shoulder. The boy's fear vanished. What a kind priest, he thought, watching the janitor leave.

"What is your name?"

"Bartholomew Garelli," said the boy. He soon told Don Bosco all about himself. His mother and father were dead, and he had no one to care for him. He worked as a bricklayer. He had never been to school, did not know anything about his

catechism, or lessons about our Catholic Faith, and he had not even made his First Holy Communion. This saddened Don Bosco the most, for his greatest joy was to receive our Lord Jesus in Holy Communion at Mass.

"Would you like to learn your catechism, if I taught you myself?" asked Don Bosco.

"Well, yes I would," answered Bartholomew with a slow smile. Don Bosco and Bartholomew said a Hail Mary together, and then Bartholomew stayed for Mass. Don Bosco prayed for Bartholomew during Mass, and asked God to bless him and help him to love and serve Him and our Blessed Mother. After Mass, Don Bosco taught him his first catechism lesson. Bartholomew liked learning about God and His wonderful ways. When it was over, Don Bosco said, "Come back next Sunday, but don't come alone. Bring your friends."

A week later, Don Bosco had nine ragged boys attend his catechism lesson! The number soon grew to thirty! Word spread from boy to boy in Turin, and more boys came each Sunday.

Don Bosco called the group "The Oratory," which means "place of prayer." The Oratory also became a place of work, study, games, and songs. Soon dozens of boys were meeting each Sunday in a church courtyard, learning their catechism and later playing games and having races. Three years later, they moved their meeting place to a country field, then to some spare rooms in an orphanage, and later they rented a farmer's wagon shed.

Each week new ones came and then kept coming. Some were as young as eight and some were as old as eighteen. Why did so many boys come to the Oratory?

At that time, there were no child labor laws, or laws against using children as workers. There also were no laws saying that children had to go to school; usually poor children received no schooling at all. Many poor children had to work at jobs to help support the family, even children as young as seven years old.

Some came from good families that were poor, and these children were lucky to have someone to care for them. Others weren't so lucky. Some came from bad families that wanted to be rid of their children, and others were orphans without a home. Many of these boys found temporary shelter in barns, sheds, or abandoned buildings. They would sleep there until someone would chase them away, and then they had to look for new shelter.

During the day, they worked many, many hours. They held such jobs as bricklayer, baker, printer, wagon driver, tailor, stable groom, janitor, factory worker, and farm laborer, and many other jobs. The boys were paid very little. Often they did not have enough money to eat, and some boys stole food. Those who were caught were put into damp, cold jail cells with hardened criminals to serve out their jail term. When a boy's work day was over, he often roamed the streets without anywhere to go. If it was wintertime, he was always cold. The boys got into fights, and sickness was a common thing. They were mistreated by their bosses and by the townspeople who didn't want them, so they often mistreated others, too.

Don Bosco knew about these "dead-end" boys, and he was determined to do something to help them. He loved them with the love of Christ, and he wanted to turn these "wild beasts" into the "flock of Christ."

Don Bosco knew that he himself was lucky when he was a boy. His mother was very devout, and loved Our Lord very much. She could not read or write, but she memorized lessons from the catechism and verses from the Bible, and taught them to her sons. Young John was very young when his father died, so Mrs. Bosco and the boys had to work very hard to keep the family farm going.

John had a strange, wonderful dream when he was a boy. He dreamed that he was in a large meadow. In the meadow, a crowd of boys were shouting, cursing, and playing roughly. John

rushed over to them, and to stop them from sinning, he began to pound on them. Then he heard a voice say, "Be gentle with them. You will not win their friendship with blows, but with kindness." He turned around and saw Jesus, who said, "Not with blows, but with kindness." He turned to look at the meadow again, and before his eyes, the boys turned into wild beasts, fighting and hurting each other. Then all of a sudden, they turned into woolly lambs, and played peacefully and happily.

Then Jesus spoke again: "Teach them right from wrong. Teach them the beauty of goodness and the ugliness of sin."

"How can I do this, Lord? I have not even been to school."

"Try, and if you keep on trying, I will help you. I will give you the best of all teachers. She was my first teacher. She will show you how to do all things with love, patience, and strength," said Jesus, looking over John's head and smiling.

54

John turned and saw Our Lady. She was beautiful, and so much more than beautiful. "I shall teach you. Someday you will understand," she said. Then she and Jesus were gone.

Young John told his mother of the dream.

"Maybe it means that you are to be a priest," she said thoughtfully. John never forgot the dream, and each day, his desire to be a priest became stronger and stronger. Mrs. Bosco and John found a kind priest who tutored him in the subjects he would need to know in the seminary, and he helped John to enter school. For many, many years, young John worked to earn money for his schooling and his lodging, since school was not near home. At different times, he worked as a tailor, house servant, barber, baker, shoe maker, and many other jobs. One person who knew him estimated that John mastered over thirty different jobs during his student days! When he worked as a janitor in a pool hall, he slept in a cubbyhole under the stairs! John was an excellent student, as well as an excellent acrobat, runner, and juggler. All of these experiences came in handy years later in teaching, training, entertaining, and taking care of "his boys."

The wagon shed that Don Bosco and his hundreds of boys rented grew later into a home, orphanage, workshop, school, and church! How? Don Bosco's method was simple. He made plans, and trusted that Our Lady Help of Christians would provide the way to complete his plans. And she always provided! The boys who no one wanted at last found a home, because Our Lady wanted them!

Don Bosco's boys soon learned their Faith, and then how to read and write, after work in the evenings. This was the world's first "night school." Those who learned quickly helped the others. Students rapidly became teachers. Some priests came to teach in their spare time, too. Prayers were frequent in the Oratory, and each day began with confessions and Mass. Some boys came to live with Don Bosco, and he designed and sewed their clothes and made their shoes for them!

Don Bosco asked his mother to come and help look after the boys. She gladly said, "Yes." She became a mother to the boys, and they all called her "Mother Margaret." Don Bosco visited all kinds of people, rich and poor, and all were glad to give money for the Oratory. Others donated equipment, supplies, and books. Soon the boys were learning ways to make an honest living. Don Bosco encouraged songs, jokes, races, and juggling among his boys. Even in his old age, he could win a foot race. He would say, "Enjoy yourself all you like, as long as you don't sin."

But not all were friendly. In Italy there were some people who were trying to destroy the Catholic Faith, and their lies misled and confused many people. Don Bosco and his boys printed booklets and magazines for Catholic youth and families that were full of good Catholic teaching. These were given out free of charge, and as a result of this, many people read them and came back to the Faith.

This made "the enemy" angry. When Don Bosco made his rounds of the city visiting the sick and needy, and looking for homeless boys to take to the Oratory, a terrible thing happened. Some men tried to kill Don Bosco! They attacked him, and were about to kill him, when all of a sudden, a large gray dog leapt at the men. His growl was ferocious, and he succeeded in chasing the men away! Then the dog escorted Don Bosco home. From that time on, whenever Don Bosco went on a dangerous mission, the gray dog mysteriously appeared and went with him. Don Bosco

called the dog, "Grigio," which is Italian for "gray one." The dog always went away when Don Bosco reached the safety of the Oratory. No one could ever discover where the dog lived. After four years, the danger passed, and it was safe again for Don Bosco to travel freely. Grigio appeared no more!

The Oratory grew, and Don Bosco's boys grew up. Many wanted to work with him, and to help children in the same way that they themselves had been helped by Don Bosco. So he started the Salesian Order, named after St. Francis de Sales, one of his favorite saints. Many of his boys who now were grown men became Salesian brothers and priests, who started new Oratories in other cities and countries. It is now one of the largest religious orders in the world! Many other boys remained in the lay state and became good men who lived in the world and spread the Gospel through their good lives. Many of them became fathers of families. They remained grateful to God all their lives for sending Don Bosco to save them!

In gratitude for Our Lady's help and guidance, Don Bosco built a basilica, or large church, in honor of her, called Our Lady Help of Christians. How much money did he have to start this big project? He had forty cents! That's all he had in his pocket when he bought the land, and the man from whom he bought the land accepted it as a "down payment"! At this time, a deadly epidemic, or contagious disease, was spreading rapidly, and people were afraid of catching the disease. Don Bosco made a strange promise to the boys who helped build the basilica, and even to any person who donated money for building supplies. The promise was this: that anyone who helped in the building of the basilica in any way would be free of the disease! An even stranger thing happened: it came true! No boy builder or person who donated to the building of the Basilica of Our Lady Help of Christians came down with the dreaded disease!

There are many, many more stories that can be told about St. John Bosco. There are stories about one of his boys, Dominic Savio, who died as a teenager, and who became a great saint. There are stories about his lifelong friendship with Mother Mary Mazzarello, a remarkable woman who cared for girls the same way that Don Bosco cared for boys, and who is also a saint. Together they began the Order of Our Lady Help of Christians and the Sisters of that order teach and serve all over the world! There are stories about his gift of "reading souls," which means that he could somehow see the sinful state of the souls of his boys, and even what sins they were guilty of committing. He used this knowledge in the confessional to help them truly cleanse their souls. There are many stories about Don Bosco's many dreams and visions which he had all his life. In those dreams, Don Bosco could see the future of the Church; he used this knowledge to help and save souls. But these tales will have to wait for another time and another story.

"Give me souls, and take away the rest!" he would say often. In his later years, he would say: "We must look for the source of all the blessings that have fallen on our works in that Hail Mary recited with young Garelli on December 8, 1841, the Feast of the Immaculate Conception, in the sacristy of the church of St. Francis of Assisi. I put all I had into my work, and the Blessed Virgin heard my prayers, and for half a century she never ceased helping me."

Don Bosco became ill and died in 1888. His last words were: "Tell all my boys that I expect to see them in Heaven."

He was canonized a saint on Easter Sunday, 1934.

Basilica of Our Lady Help of Christians in Turin, Italy

Choosing Wisely

One thing St. John Bosco helped his boys with was choosing good friends. Because we tend to act like our friends do, we want to surround ourselves with friends who will encourage us to develop good character and virtue. Study the faces on pages 59–61. The artists tried to capture certain character qualities in the faces they painted, some more obviously than others. Look them over, considering the qualities you would like in a friend and other qualities you want to avoid. Select a picture that represents to you the qualities you want in a friend. Cut out the image you chose and paste it in the first box below. Choose the character qualities you'd like your friend to have, using the list of character qualities provided or your own ideas. Write these qualities on the lines under the box. Now paste a photo of yourself in the second box. On the lines under this box, write the character qualities you think you have and also the ones you want to develop.

Good sport	Diligent	Trouble maker	Thoughtful
Jealous	Boastful	Trustworthy	Mean
Generous	Respectful	Creative	Responsible
Honest	Moody	Caring	Lazy
Cheerful	Critical	Bossy	Selfish

9

We don't need to map out every detail of our lives. God is going to throw some twists and surprises in every now and then, and we may end up in unexpected but not necessarily tragic places. We can cooperate with His grace or refuse it. Let's read about Mother Cabrini, a saint who accomplished great things in spite of some very challenging twists and turns.

Someone to Care

by Elaine Woodfield

Yolande woke up itching. It happened every morning. Scratching her skin and scalp only made it itch more. Yolande also woke up cold. She looked over at her sister, Loredana, and their friend, Mary, as both younger girls slept peacefully. Then she knew why she was so cold. The girls had pulled most of the blanket off of her onto themselves in their sleep.

"Blanket stealers," she thought as she smiled at them.

It really wasn't a blanket at all. It was a dirty, tattered sheet that someone had thrown away. Yolande had found it in a pile of trash, and took it with her. She was glad she found it, because she knew that it would help them stay warm at night. The girls decided to call it "the blanket" to remind themselves that there had once been a time that they really did sleep under a blanket. But those days were long ago.

Yolande knew why she had woken up. She reached into her pocket and checked to see that the five pennies were there. They were, and she smiled again. Four of them she had earned by shining shoes, and one she had found on the sidewalk. A lucky penny! Hadn't her mother told her that finding a lucky penny meant that something good was about to happen to you?

Yolande's eyes filled with tears. She missed her mother and father so much! They had died suddenly from sickness. It seemed so long ago.

She made her way out to Mott Street, and bought some buns at a nearby bakery with her pennies. She was glad that she and the girls would have a good breakfast.

"Five buns for five pennies," sang the baker. He put them in a bag for her. Yolande heard someone behind her in line talking.

"What a filthy little girl! And look at her hair! It's all matted! Who does she belong to?"

"No one. She's an orphan, poor thing."

"You mean she has no one to take care of her?"

"She shines shoes. That's how she takes care of herself."

"But someone has to care!"

"It's a big city with a lot of people."

"I think I know someone who will care: Sister Francesca."

Yolande took her bag and hurried out. She was

afraid that someone would separate her from her sister and Mary, and make them live apart from each other. Prison was where thieves go. And Yolande was not proud of being a thief. She stole pieces of fruit and bread from the pushcarts and marketplace stalls when she and the girls hadn't eaten anything at all for days.

But as she walked back "home," the rhythm of her feet made a rhyme in her head.

"Sister Francesca, someone to care. Sister Francesca, someone to care," she said softly, over and over.

She went through the doorway and down the stairs. The girls were awake, and they grinned and clapped their hands when she showed them

the bakery buns. They ate them very slowly, as hungry people do, to savor every crumb and to make their meal last longer.

What was their "home"?

It was a coal bin in an unused basement!

They lived in New York City in 1889. In those days, furnaces and fireplaces burned chunks of black coal to heat buildings. Each day, someone in each home or building shoveled coal from the coal bin into the furnace to keep it burning brightly. Some buildings were heated by fireplaces, so someone shoveled coal from the bin into a bucket and took it upstairs for the fire. Meals were cooked on coal burning stoves, too.

Where did the coal come from?

It was mined from the ground and brought to the cities and towns. Each week or two, a coal truck came to each building and poured chunks of black coal down a coal chute, or slide, that was built into each building. The coal landed in the basement coal bin the size of a small room.

Yolande and Loredana had found a bin that wasn't used anymore in the basement of a tenement, or slum apartment building, after their parents died. Mary's parents were Chinese and when they died, she wandered the streets. Loredana found her, and took her to live with them as an adopted sister. So here amid dusty pieces of coal lived three little girls!

New York City in 1889 was big, noisy, busy, and sometimes dangerous. It was crowded with buildings, short and tall, new and old, and the buildings were crowded with people. Most of all, it was crowded with immigrants, or people who had traveled from other countries to America to make new lives for themselves. The poor people of Europe heard many stories of wealth and success to be found in America. They heard that jobs were plentiful, houses were big, farmland was fruitful, and life was easier. The life of a poor person in Europe, and also in Asia and Africa, was a hard one, so many came by boat to America. They hoped only for a better life.

Unfortunately, what many of the immigrants found in New York City was another hard life. Jobs were plentiful if you were willing to work in a factory for twelve hours or more a day and make barely enough to feed yourself. Women and even children worked long hours in unsafe factories. Houses were big only for the rich. The immigrants crowded into old unsafe tenements with no plumbing because it was all they could afford. It was not unusual for ten, or even twenty people to live in one tenement room! By and by, the immigrants were able to make better lives for themselves, but this took time. They had come from many countries: Poland, Ireland, Germany, Croatia, Russia, Greece, China, Romania, to name a very few.

Yolande's parents were from Italy. Most immigrants could not speak English, and so it was hard for them to better themselves quickly in America. Many immigrants could not find a priest who spoke their language, and so many fell away from their Catholic Faith. This Faith alone could console and guide them in their difficulties, and so this loss of Faith was the immigrant's greatest tragedy.

Disease and death were commonplace. Dirty and homeless orphans were commonplace too.

Yolande spent the day trying to shine shoes on Mott Street. She called out, "Shoeshine! Shoeshine!" in Italian, the only language she knew. Mott Street was an Italian neighborhood. All the shopkeepers and neighbors knew the language. But few people were interested in shiny shoes that day, and Yolande had only three cents and a hoarse voice for all her trouble.

The sun was going down when Yolande arrived home.

"Guess what?" Loredana asked her.

"I don't know. What?" asked Yolande with a yawn.

"Mary found a penny on the sidewalk!" Loredana shouted happily. She and Mary spent their day looking for spare change on the streets and sidewalks.

"Ah! So this is where you live?" said a soft, womanly voice in Italian. Yolande looked up, and looking back at her were the kindest eyes she had ever seen.

"Who are you?" she gasped in surprise.

"Sister Francesca Cabrini, my child. I have come to take you home." Sister was dressed in black, with a black veil over her hair. She walked over to the younger girls and picked them both up, one on each arm, as if they were as light as two feathers.

"But this is our home," said Yolande stubbornly. Tears sprang up in her eyes, and she didn't know why.

"I have come to take you home to your mother and father," said Sister Francesca.

"But they're in Heaven with God, Sister!"

"You have a new mother and father now. Our Lord Jesus Himself will be your Father, and I and my Sisters will be your mothers," Sister Francesca said softly.

"Where will we live?" asked Loredana. Mary gazed at Sister adoringly. The girls never knew how much of the language Mary understood, but they knew that she was smart.

"You will live in our new Home for Orphans. Come! It's a long walk to Fifty-Ninth Street!" sang Sister Francesca. She held the girls by the hand as they walked along Mott Street, then turned down another street, then another.

Yolande felt as if she were in a dream. She couldn't stop asking questions.

"Will we sleep in a real bed?"

Sister laughed, and Yolande thought that her laughter sounded like music.

"Yes, my child, in a real bed with real sheets that are clean and white."

"Will we eat every day?"

"Three meals every day."

"THREE MEALS?" Yolande and Loredana shouted together. They couldn't believe it!

"Yes, and you will go to school."

"SCHOOL?" the girls shouted again. "But Sister, school is only for rich children," said Yolande.

"No, my child, school is for all my children, and none of them are rich."

All of a sudden, Sister stopped walking, knelt on the pavement so that her face was level with the faces of the girls, and looked steadily into the eyes of each girl.

"Children, I have a question to ask each of you. Do you know what kind of child you are?" she asked, peering into each dirty face.

Yolande could not look at Sister. She was ashamed that sometimes she had taken food that wasn't hers, and looked at her feet. A tear ran down her cheek, but she didn't notice.

Sister took Yolande's face in her two hands, and finally Yolande looked into the kind eyes that were as blue as the sky.

"You are a child of God," she said with a beautiful smile. Her two hands touched Loredana's face and she repeated, "You are a child of God," and she took Mary's face too, and repeated, "You are a child of God."

"I am a child of God," whispered Yolande. She was scarcely able to believe it herself.

"You are so precious to Him that He sent His Son Jesus to die on the cross to save you, my children," said Sister.

"But I'm a thief," blurted out Yolande. "I took food when we were so hungry. And besides, no one wants us."

"And do you know about the very first person that the Lord Jesus took to Heaven after He died?"

"No, Sister."

"We call him Dismas, the Good Thief. He was crucified next to Jesus, but he was sorry for his sins. He believed in the mercy of Jesus, and as a reward for his faith, Jesus took him to Heaven first!" said Sister as they walked on.

"Really?" asked Yolande.

"You are just as precious to Him. You are so precious that the Lord Jesus makes Himself available for you to visit Him. That's part of the surprise."

"What surprise?" asked the girls excitedly. Loredana began to skip as she walked.

"Our Lord lives at our Home for Orphans. We visit Him every day."

"How?"

"We have a chapel in our Home. Jesus in the Blessed Sacrament lives there in the tabernacle."

"What's a chapel, Sister?"

Sister Francesca laughed. Mary's eyes never left Sister's face, and she smiled at Sister's laugh. "I see that I have many wonderful things to teach you," she said. They turned, and went into a big building.

"We are home," she said. Just inside the doorway was a statue of a Man dressed in red and white robes. Yolande and the girls could see His heart. It was circled with thorny branches, and looked as if it were on fire with yellow flames. On top of the heart, in the middle of the flames, was a cross.

"Who is this, Sister?"

"This is a statue of the Sacred Heart of Jesus. He is the Master of this house, my spouse Jesus Christ," said Sister Francesca. Yolande remembered her mother telling her that nuns were special because they were the brides of Christ.

"What does this heart mean? Why is it on fire?"

"His Sacred Heart on fire is the symbol for the burning love He has for us, a love that would stop at nothing to save us from the horror of sin, the love that made Him die on the cross for love of us."

"What are these thorny branches, Sister?"

"Those are our sins, which wound His Heart more terribly than the crown of thorns that He wore on the cross."

"You mean He loves even me?" asked Yolande.

"You most of all because you took care of your sisters," said Sister Francesca, giving her shoulders a hug.

"Always remember that the Sacred Heart of Jesus loves you. This way, you will stop at nothing to love Him back," Sister continued.

"Is that why you came for us?" asked Loredana.

"Yes, my child, to love Him back by loving you, His precious children," said Sister with a smile. "You have understood well."

She led them to a large kitchen where two sisters and some older girls were putting dishes away.

"Welcome," they all said, smiling. One girl put her broom away and got them some bread and milk. Yolande ate and ate, so hungry was she.

After a while, Sister Francesca took them down a long hallway to a large room with a huge white container on the floor that was big enough for all three girls to get into. The walls were shiny, and the room echoed with every sound they made.

"Now my work begins," Sister said, smiling. Yolande wasn't sure what she meant. "Off with these clothes," said Sister, undressing them.

"NO!" screamed the girls. The room echoed.

Photo of Mother Cabrini

"We'll be cold!" They struggled, but Sister removed the filthy, bug-infested clothing. Another Sister poured warm water from kettles and pots into the bathtub until it was almost full — she smiled at the commotion the girls made.

"Now into the tub," said Sister gently, a screaming girl under each arm.

"NO! NO! What are you doing?" they screamed as Sister put them in the bath of warm water. She returned to Yolande, who screamed the loudest, even after she realized that the water was pleasant. Sister Francesca used washcloths and lots of soap to scrub the screaming girls.

"It hurts! Why are you doing this?" sobbed Yolande. "We thought you were a kind lady!"

The girls had been without a bath for so long that they really didn't remember what one was like! Sister Francesca patiently washed and rinsed, washed and rinsed each struggling girl. Soon the girls stopped fussing. By and by, all the dirt and grime came off. The girls were now clean.

Sister combed and cut each girl's mop of hopelessly snarled hair until a comb ran smoothly through it, then she dressed the girls in clean, crisp nightgowns. She tucked them into bed herself, and each girl threw her arms around Sister Francesca and said "I love you!" so grateful were they. Yolande could scarcely remember how wonderfully warm a real blanket on a real bed felt. After Sister said their prayers with them, since they had forgotten how to say them, Yolande snuggled into her pillow. As she drifted off to sleep, she remembered her lucky penny that she had found yesterday.

"Sister Francesca, someone to care," she murmured over and over, the rhythm of the words soothing her to sleep.

Who was Sister Francesca?

Francesca Cabrini was born in the Lombardy region of Italy on July 15, 1850; on that day, a flock of white doves flew in circles over the Cabrini home! She was the youngest of a large, very devout Catholic family. She was a sickly child, and was in frail health all her life. The Cabrini family was close-knit, loving, and happy. In the evenings, Papa Cabrini would read to the family out loud from a book of true missionary stories. Francesca loved to hear about the missions, and dreamed of lands far away.

When she was seven, she received the Sacrament of Confirmation. It was a day that changed her life forever. She gazed upon the statue of the Sacred Heart of Jesus, and was anointed with the sacred chrism by the bishop.

"The moment of the anointing of the sacred chrism, I felt that which can never be described. From that moment I was no longer of the earth. My heart began to grow through space ever with purest joy. I cannot tell why, but I knew the Holy Ghost had come to me," she recalled years later. From that moment, two desires burned in her heart. She wanted to be a Bride of Christ, and she wanted to be a missionary so that she could spread God's love everywhere.

Francesca trained to become a schoolteacher like her sister, and she applied to become a nun, but she was turned down because of her poor health. A holy priest advised her to start her own order of nuns. And that's what she did!

But first she needed to prepare herself. Her bishop sent her to work at a place called the House of Providence. It was an orphanage for girls owned by a certain woman who received money from the nearby parish for the upkeep of each orphan girl.

What no one knew was that the woman was very cruel. She kept most of the money herself and she made the girls live with dirt, hard work, and ignorance. Francesca loved the girls. She cleaned them up, scrubbed the rooms, and suffered under the insults of the cruel woman. She taught the girls, and did household chores with them. Each night, she told the girls stories of the Catholic Faith, and they sang hymns together before they went to sleep.

The girls blossomed under Francesca's loving care. And Francesca herself grew in love for the Sacred Heart of Jesus. After a long while, others discovered that the woman was being cruel to the orphan girls and to Francesca. Then Francesca was put in charge of the House of Providence!

After six years, Francesca took vows of poverty, chastity, and obedience, and became Sister Francesca, Bride of Christ. She began her religious order, called the Missionaries of the Sacred Heart, and many of the orphan girls joined her and became nuns, too.

Sister Francesca and the Sisters begged money to buy an old monastery, and took in orphans to care for. When the building needed to be enlarged, the Sisters could not afford to hire many bricklayers. One of the Sisters had an idea. Her father had been a bricklayer, and she had helped him at his work many times when she had been a girl. She remembered what she had learned about bricklaying, and she taught the other Sisters. So the Sisters did most of the bricklaying on the building addition themselves!

Sister Francesca's lifelong method was simple: she trusted fully in the Providence of God to provide complete help for her, and then she went ahead with her plans. She and the Sisters went from door to door asking for money and food for the orphans from neighbors and shopkeepers, and they always got what they needed.

In this way, Sister Francesca opened another orphanage, then another, until there were seven houses of her nuns in Italy!

She went to Rome and spoke with Pope Leo XIII herself, telling him of her desire to be a missionary to the people of the Far East.

"You must be a missionary to the West," he told her. News of the immigrants' plight reached him, and he knew that Sister Francesca and the Sacred Heart of Jesus could bring many immigrants back to the Faith and out of despair. Pope Leo XIII became her lifelong friend and supporter.

So off to America she went! In New York City she and the Sisters went up and down stairways, visiting tenements, nursing the sick, giving out food, begging from all who could spare money or food, helping the dying, and collecting homeless orphans. She spoke to dozens of poor immigrants each day. They were God's own children, and she revered them and served them. She begged among the poor for those poorer still; she soon

discovered that poor people are often the most generous givers of all!

She took Yolande with her when she went begging on Mott Street. The shopkeepers were amazed to see her so clean and happy, and they gave the Sisters even more so that they could work the same miracle with more orphans.

Yolande was happy to be going to school now, and gratefully she polished the Sisters' shoes at night! But most of all, she was glad to have God for her Father and the Sisters for her Mothers!

Sister Francesca was now called Mother Cabrini. She worked her miracle in many different places. She founded a school in Nicaragua, Central

America. She helped the downtrodden Italian immigrants in New Orleans, Louisiana. She helped the miners in Colorado, and founded hospitals in Chicago and New York.

Tending the sick was something that Mother Cabrini found distasteful, until she had a dream. She saw a beautiful lady in blue with her sleeves rolled up, changing bloody bandages cheerfully and gently tending the sick. She realized that this was the Virgin Mary, and she realized that no service of those in need should be distasteful to her. From then on, she always served the sick with calm cheerfulness.

Mother Cabrini crossed the ocean a total of twenty-five times, even though she was deathly afraid of water travel. She traveled to Chile, crossed the cold Andes Mountains on mule-back, and arrived in Argentina. She traveled to Brazil, Panama, France, California, and Spain. Everywhere she founded convents of nuns and began orphanages, schools, and sometimes hospitals. She wrote letters to her Sisters all the time and they wrote to her with news and requests for advice. She became an American citizen, too.

Near the end of her life, she said to a sad sister: "Child, you have troubles? With fifty houses to think about, I have none! Let us abandon ourselves to God, my dear daughter, let us be conducted and guided by Him, let us do His Will, and then our faces will not be sad, but always serene and radiant."

She died in 1917, in Columbus Hospital in Chicago, which she herself had founded years before. At the time of her death, there were over one thousand nuns in her order, five thousand orphans being cared for in her orphanages, thousands of students in her schools, and hundreds of thousands of patients that had been served in her hospitals. Her lifelong motto was, "I can do all things, in Him who strengthens me."

Francesca Cabrini was beatified in 1938, and she was proclaimed a saint in 1946. She is the first American saint, and is called, in our language, St. Frances Cabrini.

Missionary of the Smile

We may not be able to travel the world doing what Mother Cabrini did, but there is plenty we can do in our own family, neighborhood, and parish. First, re-read the story and notate all the places in the world that Mother Cabrini traveled to, setting up new hospitals and orphanages. Using the map on the next page, place a colorful sticker on each location to mark her travels. Next, turn the map over and each time you've practiced your missionary smile, place a sticker on the location.

For example, say that this week you need to go to the dentist to have a cavity filled. Instead of frowning or pouting, put on your best smile. (Don't forget to smile at the dentist, too!) Write "dentist" on one of the buildings on your map and add a sticker.

What if your mom serves your least favorite food for dinner tonight? You think, "Ugh." Will you frown or wear a smile?

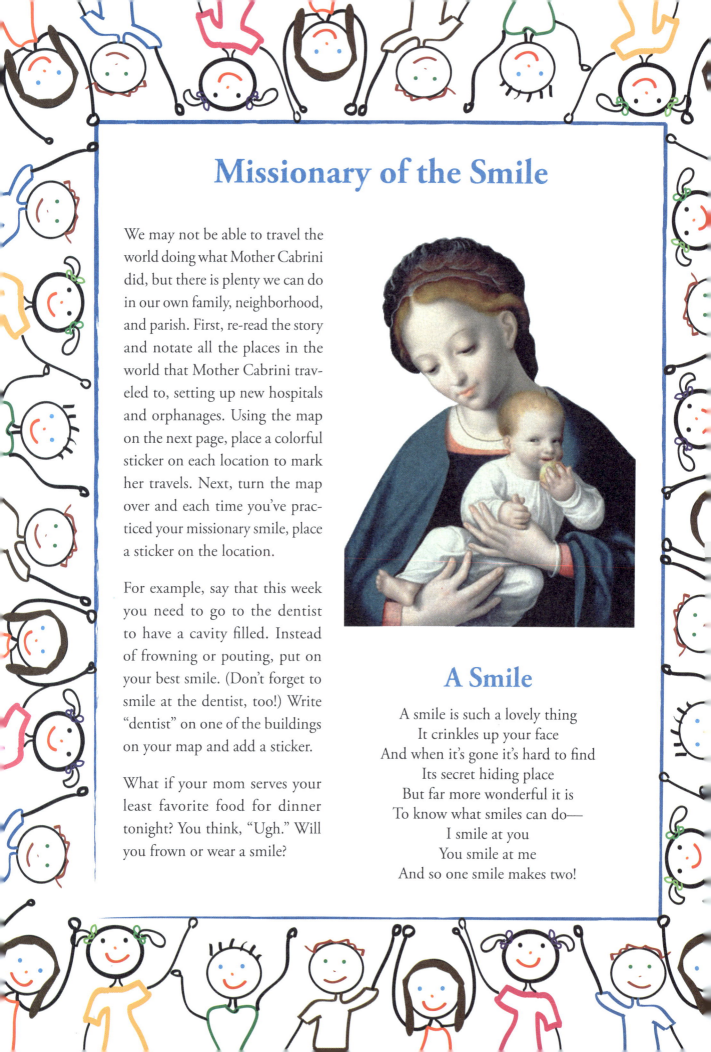

A Smile

A smile is such a lovely thing
It crinkles up your face
And when it's gone it's hard to find
Its secret hiding place
But far more wonderful it is
To know what smiles can do—
I smile at you
You smile at me
And so one smile makes two!

Mother Cabrini's Travels

My Missionary Travels

10

Sometimes God loves us too much to permit life to go the way we planned. He has something much better in mind for us. We may not immediately see how His plan is better. Sometimes the first challenge is simply to trust that He does love us. Challenges are perfect opportunities to be creative, whether they are physical, mental, or spiritual challenges. Let's read about Mary, a girl who creatively changed a challenge into a gift.

Mary's Sacrifice

There were four children in the Beresford family: Dermot, Brian, Mary, and Kathleen. The children looked upon their parents as the best and greatest people in the world.

Mr. Beresford sat at the breakfast table on a certain morning in spring, and looked at the bright faces on either side of him. Mr. Beresford's hair had begun to turn gray lately. Mary, so lovingly observant, noticed that the wrinkles near his eyes made a network of fine lines. He said grace and then said, "I have news for you, children."

"My business ventures in the West have gone wrong. And Doctor Jarvis says that I shall die, unless I move to the country as soon as possible. When I sell this house I may have enough money to buy a farm. I hoped, as you know, to send you to a good school for several years; but I cannot do it now. Well, well—how do you like the idea of farming?"

Dermot said nothing. He hung his head, and if he had been a younger boy, a tear would have dropped into his oatmeal. It was a great disappointment.

Brian, on the contrary, was much relieved. He often said to himself that it was a shame for his father to be growing gray-haired over old law books in an office, while Dermot and he studied or played. He said he wanted to work.

Mary's eyes brightened. "And I can really help Mother! Oh, I think farming will be nice!"

Mrs. Beresford shook her head. "We shall be very poor."

"Why, Mother," said Mary, "haven't you told us often that if we were contented and good, poverty made no difference? We shall all be together. Isn't that enough?"

"It is a great sacrifice for you all to leave this fine house and the lively city," said Mr. Beresford, "but I must ask it of you. It is my duty to save my life and health until you are able to take care of yourselves. I know you will all help me."

Dermot went to his father and put his arms around his neck. "Dear Father," he said, with tears in his eyes, "I will do anything for your sake."

"Come, let's be cheerful and talk over our plans."

Mary went upstairs after breakfast. She drew from a wardrobe a pretty white gown. It was soft, and here and there among its folds rested brilliant silver lace. She looked at it sadly. It had been given to her on her birthday. She had not yet worn it, and her father had promised to let her invite as many of her friends as she chose, in honor of his birthday, which would be late in May. But now that was all over. She could not remind her father of his promise.

The sunlight on the pretty gown made the silver lace glisten like the reflections of light on a rippling stream. The tears came into her eyes. She felt tempted to ask her father; he would understand and let her have a celebration on his birthday. She knew he would! But then he was so worried about other things. And then the expense! She heard his step sounding in his study. She would just run in and ask him. It would be so nice to wear that pretty dress. She made a movement toward the door.

Was she selfish? she asked herself. She looked at the Madonna and Child that stood on the pedestal in one corner of her room. Her mother had often told her that in times of difficulty she ought to pray and to try to model her conduct on that of the Blessed Virgin. She thought of her father's bowed head and the wrinkles around his eyes. She prayed. Then, with a sigh, she put the soft gown back into its box and cried a little.

She had just wiped her eyes when a flutter was heard on the stairs. She opened the door and a girl about her own age came in and hugged her hard. It was Alice Howe. Alice moved with as much vivacity as she could, considering that her dress was very tight, and that she had a little dog which she led by a string. She threw herself into a chair, while the dog sniffed around the room.

"Oh, dear!" she said, in an affected imitation of what she thought to be an English tone of voice, "I'm quite too awfully tired. You really ought to have an elevator in this big house. I've just run in to ask you to my luncheon on the 28th. It will be quite lovely. Mamma has ordered favors for twenty girls, and Papa has promised me that the flowers shall be something superb. You must come, and wear your new dress."

Alice, a pleasant looking girl, with wide open blue eyes and yellow hair, was, unfortunately, spoiled. Her parents were too busy with other and less important matters to give her much attention.

Mary's manner was very simple compared with the airs of Alice; but Mary could look one directly in the face, with a clear and honest gaze.

"You are very kind, Alice," Mary answered, "but I think we will be out of town by the 28th."

"So soon! When are you going? It's just the time for Atlantic City, before the crush begins—"

"No, no," said Mary, hastily, "we are not going away for pleasure. Poor Father is not well, and we are going into the country to live."

"Not for good!" cried Alice.

"Yes."

"You can't mean it. What, are you to give up the riding club, and the party you promised us? You certainly are crazy, Mary."

"The truth is," said Mary, with an effort and a slight blush, "we're too poor to live here."

Alice leaned back in her chair and laughed.

"This is quite too awfully funny! Fancy"—she said 'fawncy'—"living in a house like this! Papa often does the same thing, whenever I want him to buy me anything pretty. But Mamma and I don't mind it! Poof! The idea! It's just your papa's talk!"

"No," said Mary, gravely, "Father always means what he says. We shall all have to work hard on a farm somewhere."

"What!" cried Alice, "you don't mean it! Oh, this is quite too dreadfully, awfully horrible, you churn the butter and milk the cows, feed the pigs and gather potatoes! Oh, my dear, your father can't be so awfully cruel! And you'll have no chance of wearing your new dress on a farm! Come now, you do not mean it?"

"Father said, this very morning, we must go away and live very carefully," Mary answered, with an effort. "I suppose if one is poor, one may be good and contented, and nice, if one tries."

"Impossible!" Alice said, running her fingers through her bangs to show a diamond ring she wore. "Poor people never can be nice. Just to think of living in a little house with no servants. Poor people are always nasty."

"Our Lord was poor. And the Blessed Virgin was poor."

Alice was silent for an instant. "Oh, that was a long time ago. Don't preach, Mary, please. Just think of it, this morning, almost before I was up, Mother came and asked me if I had a white dress I didn't want. I was quite paralyzed by the question, for Mamma knows very well that I want everything I have. It seems that a poor woman, who lives behind our house, had the impudence to ask Mamma for a dress, so that her daughter could make her First Holy Communion dressed in white, like the other girls. To be fair, she only wanted to borrow one, and having heard that I went to the convent school, she thought Mamma might lend her one of mine! Fancy! She said it would be a great favor, as she could not afford to buy a white dress. Did you ever hear of such a thing? I was very angry!"

Mary was silent. A slight color came to her face.

"You aggravating girl," continued Alice, "you won't give me a bit of sympathy. Imagine your laundry woman asking you for a gown. I guess you'd be very angry, too."

"No," said Mary, "I would not."

"What virtue!" cried Alice sarcastically. "I should like to see you lend her one of your white dresses, the new one, for instance!"

Mary walked over to the bookcase and looked at the pretty rows of gilded books. Alice's words had struck home.

"The girl's name is Anna Doran and she lives in Wilbert's Court. There, my dear friend! Don't preach to me unless you practice what you preach. To change the subject, I shall have my new fan painted for your party."

"Alice, believe me, there will be no more parties

for me. We are poor now, and we shall all have to work."

Alice went close to Mary and looked into her face. "Are you really in earnest?"

"Indeed I am!"

"Bosh!" cried Alice, "Come live with me. You can have half my room. Let the boys be poor if they want to. You come and live with us."

Mary laughed. "Oh, Alice, how silly you are! How could I leave my family? I must help them. I shall study hard, if I have to stay up all night."

Alice threw herself back in her chair and laughed. She mimicked Mary over and over again, with much apparent enjoyment.

"Oh, dear," she cried at last, "you will kill me!"

Alice saw a dangerous sparkle in Mary's eye, for Mary had by nature what is called a "temper," but she had been taught to control it.

"Well, good-bye, Mary. If you will take summer boarders when you go on the farm, I'll come. But I think it's real mean about your party. And all the girls will talk it over and say unkind things. It will be quite too awfully foolish!"

Alice kissed Mary on both cheeks and then bounded away.

Left alone, Mary knelt down near the wide window seat and cried. All the girls who had often entertained Mary would say she was too mean to keep her promise about the birthday party. It did look mean, Mary admitted to herself. She had talked so much about the party and her new gown.

She said to herself that she would wear it; she would speak to her father and tell him that he ought to give her a last party. How lovely the

dress would look, if she could only wear it and have one more good time, in spite of everything.

Somehow or other, just then, she calmed. It would not be serving God to worry her dear father just now and, perhaps, coax him into spending money for luxuries that he really needed for necessities.

If she could only wear that lovely white dress, just once! But no, she was a poor girl now.

Alice Howe's visit had disturbed her. It had made her uneasy and discontented. The incident of the child whose mother wanted to borrow the white dress came into her mind. Ought she to make a sacrifice and give up this beautiful gown?

She ran down to the sitting room to find her mother. She was busy at her small desk attending to her correspondence.

"Yes, Mary?" she said.

"Mother, Alice Howe has just been telling me of a poor girl who has no dress to wear at her First Holy Communion, and I thought—" Mrs. Beresford looked a little troubled. "You know, my dear, we are not as we used to be, and I am afraid I have no white fabric that would do for such a dress. And I don't think you have any that would suit."

"Oh, yes, I have," said Mary, eagerly. "My new one!"

Mrs. Beresford smiled. "Where do these people live—the people Alice spoke of?"

"Back in the court. Their name is Doran."

Mrs. Beresford's face brightened. "Oh yes, a very respectable family. The father is in the hospital. The mother did some work for me a while ago. You can go over. I think, though, that if you give the young girl your dress, you had better remove the silver lace. It would look conspicuous and out of place."

"Very well, Mother. Can I go now?"

Mrs. Beresford smiled, and Mary ran off to get her hat.

****

The Dorans were very poor. Dick, Anna's elder brother, lay on a lounge in their little parlor, unable to move. He had been thrown from a wagon and injured. Mrs. Doran went to people's homes to wash and iron their laundry. Anna was obliged to stay at home, to nurse Dick.

These days Anna was unusually silent. Generally, she was very happy and cheerful, but today her fits of quietness made her brother wonder.

Anna had a deep grief in her heart. She had only two worn and patched dresses. They might be made to do in the street, for they were always neat and clean, but they were so old from hard wear that she could not wear either of them in church on the great day. Oh, if she only had a white dress! It was useless to wish for such an impossible thing. Her mother could scarcely get sufficient money to pay the rent and Dick's medical bills.

Dick would have given her a dress, if he were well and able to earn money. And her dear father could not do it either. They had never let father know how poor they were. He was looking forward to seeing Anna come to his bedside at the hospital, in her white dress, after the function at the church. Tears came into Anna's eyes when she thought of his disappointment.

Her mother had thought of asking Mrs. Howe for an old dress of Alice's. We know how that turned out. The time was so near, and nobody would help her to do the thing she most wanted—though it was a little thing! She saw many girls in the street carelessly wearing white dresses, and she had to pray hard to keep herself from envying them. While Dick slept, Anna took out her rosary and prayed that she might be allowed to make her First Holy Communion with the others.

"After all," she thought, "Our dear Lord will know best." And then the fear and anxiety left her. She busied herself with arranging a few flowers, which were sent to Dick by a neighboring market woman. There was a knock on the door. Anna opened the door, and Mary stood on the threshold, smiling a little.

"May I come in?"

"Certainly," answered Anna, recognizing her guest, for she had seen her at church, "you are Miss Beresford, are you not?"

"I am Mary Beresford." And, catching sight of the covered figure on the sofa asked, "Is your brother sick?"

"Yes," said Anna, "he is better now, he's asleep."

Anna gave her a chair, and as she noticed how neat and tasteful her guest's dress was, she wished her dress were less shabby. Then the remembrance of her own trouble, concerning a dress, came to her and she sighed.

Mary's quick ear caught the sigh. "I must tell you why I came; I hope you will not be offended. I was told that you were to make your First Holy Communion with the others in a few days."

"Not with the others, I'm afraid."

An eager question rose to Mary's lips, but she did not speak it. She waited for Anna to go on, but Anna paused. Mary felt it difficult to mention the dress, now that she had come.

Suddenly, Dick, who had been dozing and was not aware that a stranger was present, spoke, "If I were rich, Anna, do you know what I'd do? Why, I'd just buy you a new dress, so that you could look like the other girls."

"Hush Dick, Miss Beresford is here."

Dick looked up and smiled at Mary. He was very pale; but his half-open eyes, his red hair, and even his weak voice expressed good nature. Dick nodded toward Mary and then relapsed into sleep.

"I came to ask you if I might give you a dress I have," said Mary, plunging into the subject in desperation, "I haven't worn it, and if you would please take it, I would be obliged."

Anna could scarcely take in the words.

"It is a nice white dress, and I think it will fit you."

Anna hid her face in her hands, and Mary saw tears trickling through her fingers.

"I am so sorry—I hope you are not offended…"

"Offended!" cried Anna, taking away her hands and looking at Mary with tear-filled eyes. "You don't know how happy you have made me! It seemed so dreadful not to be able to go with the others. And Father would be so disappointed if I did not go in white. Oh, dear, if you will only lend me your dress, I shall be very, very happy!"

Mary's face glowed with pleasure. "I want to give it to you, if you will take it. You are just about my size. I'll send it over this afternoon. I must go now. Good-bye!"

Mary hurried away to escape Anna's thanks. All her forebodings were forgotten—all her desire to wear her pretty dress was gone—she almost ran home. She met Alice Howe coming out of a candy shop, with a big box of chocolate bonbons. Alice called to her, but Mary shook her head, as she was eager to get home.

It didn't take her long to remove the silver lace from the white gown. She did it, singing cheerfully. She knew now how sweet it is to make others happy. Her mother gave her some thin fabric for a veil for Anna, and some blue ribbon. In the afternoon, Mary put the precious dress in its box, and, with the veil and ribbon wrapped in tissue paper, went with her little sister, Kathleen, to Wilbert's Court.

Kathleen talked quite happily to Dick while Anna tried on the dress, and Mary critically inspected it in the kitchen. A little pinning and a few stitches made the dress just right.

Anna forgot her bashfulness in the excitement of the process, and Mary had so many suggestions to make, that she talked a lot and very fast—an unusual thing with her. At last Anna stood arrayed in the new dress. Dick almost jumped from his sofa in delight.

Smiling and blushing, Anna let them admire. While they were still admiring, Mrs. Doran entered, tired and worn out, laden with brooms, brushes, and a bucket. She understood the situation at a glance.

She sat down on a chair near the door and looked at Anna. Then she looked at Mary and tried to speak. "God bless you, my dear," she tried to say and her voice choked. She began to sob. "You don't know what a kindness you've done."

When Mrs. Doran had wiped her eyes, she asked Mary to have tea with the family. Mary said she would, partly because she feared to offend Mrs. Doran, and partly because she wanted to see how poor people live. She expected to be very poor herself, and she wanted to know how the poor lived.

Anna was not long in getting tea ready. A round table was moved over near Dick's sofa, so that he could sit up and have his tea, too. A teapot and five cups and saucers were produced and put on the white cloth, with some bread and raspberry jam. Mary, who expected to see tin cups and perhaps wooden spoons, was pleasantly surprised. Everything was as clean and as shining as at home. Kathleen laughed and chatted away, and enjoyed her tea very much. After a pleasant hour, Mary and Kathleen said good-bye.

In the evening, Mary told her father all about her visit. He was very much interested. "And so you gave away your new dress?"

"It wasn't much loss to me, Father, I didn't need it."

"Well, my dear," said her father, smiling—how that smile on his pale face cheered her in years to come—"I say with all my heart: May God reward you, my child!"

Adapted from the book titled,
How They Worked Their Way
written in 1892 by Maurice Francis Egan

Creativity Thieves

Identify creativity thieves in your life! These are objects, habits, or activities that squash ideas and opportunities. Television and the internet can be creativity thieves when we overuse them. They provide us with lots of information, but too much stimulation can kill our creativity just as quickly as too little stimulation can. Negative comments, too many toys, too many scheduled activities, and not enough empty space threaten our creativity. Too much clutter in our lives takes up our time. We can't add more time, but we can get rid of the clutter. What do you need to do within your own bedroom and study area to get rid of clutter, create empty space, and leave room for creative opportunities?

Color the image below that best represents your room as it looks right now. In the lines provided below, list what you need to do to rid yourself of creativity thieves. Start working on your list today!

_____   _____

_____   _____

_____   _____

_____   _____

_____   _____

11

God wants us to use creativity to meet the ordinary and extraordinary challenges that confront us. Recognizing a challenge is a sign of maturity, even if you never succeed in solving it completely in this life. If a challenge seems impossible, ask a parent to help you "re-size" it. How would the challenge look if you were a giant, an ant, an artist, an athlete, the President of the United States, a saint? Can you "walk around" the challenge and see it from different mental angles? Can you get "inside" a challenge and look out? Let's read about the physical challenges the saint in our next story faced. Although he was severely handicapped, Blessed Herman's creativity seemed to know no bounds.

The Salve Regina

by Elaine Woodfield

The candle seemed to get brighter as the room got darker. The monk stared at the gently dancing flame, a peaceful smile on his face. He looked beyond it to his room's picture of Our Lady, and he smiled even more.

"I hope I have served you well today, my Lady, and given glory to God," he whispered. He looked down at the manuscript that he had finally finished composing that day. It was a prayer in honor of Our Lady. What prayer was it?

It was one of the most beautiful prayers ever written, called the "Salve Regina," or "Hail, Holy Queen."

Brother Herman prayed it again himself silently as he reread his manuscript. Just then he heard a soft knock, and another Brother entered, smiling at Brother Herman. He started to work right away and worked smoothly at his tasks because he had done this many times before. What did he do?

He got Brother Herman ready for sleep. Brother Herman was so deformed and his muscles were so contracted that he could not walk or move out of his bed without assistance. He spent most of his life bedridden.

Brother Herman first came to the monastery when he was seven years old. His parents realized that his mind was as brilliant as his body was disabled, and they knew the best place for him was the Benedictine Monastery on Lake Constance, Switzerland, where he could develop his mind with the scholarship for which the Benedictines were famous. He was professed as a monk at age twenty, and he used his fine mind in the service of God.

Brother Herman was an extraordinary man. He was famous throughout all of Europe as one of the most brilliant and gifted men of his time. He had written a treatise on mathematics and astronomy, a chronicle of world history, and religious poetry that taught the truths of the Faith, too. He made astronomical instruments to better read the positions and paths of the stars, and he was also known as a maker of musical instruments.

His finest works, however, are his prayers, especially the "Salve Regina."

How could he know, that certain night, how much honor he would give to Our Lady and how much glory he would give to God by writing this one prayer? For this prayer has been recited at the end of the Rosary by countless people for almost a thousand years! Religious orders vie with each other in claiming it as their special favorite. Martyrs for the Catholic Faith have gone to their deaths with this prayer on their lips, and it has been recited at countless bedsides of the dying in order to comfort and strengthen them. Dozens of musical composers have set this prayer to music. Countless are the favors in the lives of men, women, and children who have recited this wonderful prayer:

Hail, Holy Queen, Mother of mercy, our life, our sweetness, and our hope!

To thee do we cry, poor banished children of Eve, to thee do we send up our sighs, mourning and weeping in this valley of tears.

Turn, then, most gracious advocate, thine eyes of mercy towards us, and after this, our exile, show unto us the blessed fruit of thy womb, Jesus!
O clement, O loving, O sweet Virgin Mary!
V. Pray for us, O Holy Mother of God.
R. That we may be made worthy of the promises of Christ.

If only Brother Herman could have seen all the glory and honor that would be given to God by his prayer. But perhaps he has. He had a great desire for Heaven, as he wrote:

"The whole of this present world and all that belongs to it—yes, this mortal life itself—has become mean and wearisome, and on the other hand the world to come, that shall not pass, and that eternal life have become so unspeakably desirable and dear that I hold all these passing things as light as thistledown."

Brother Herman combined a brilliant mind and a disabled body with a pure and strong love for Our Lord and Our Lady. Blessed Herman of Reichenau died in 1054, and his feast day is September 25.

Herman the Cripple

by William Hart Hurlbut, M.D.

I am least among the low,
I am weak and I am slow;
I can neither walk nor stand,
Nor hold a spoon in my own hand.

Like a body bound in chain,
I am on a rack of pain,
But He is God who made me so,
that His mercy I should know.

Brothers do not weep for me!
Christ, the Lord, has set me free.
All my sorrows He will bless;
Pain is not unhappiness.

From my window I look down
To the streets of yonder town,
Where the people come and go,
Reap the harvest that they sow.

Like a field of wheat and tares,
Some are lost in worldly cares;
There are hearts as black as coal,
There are cripples of the soul.

Brothers do not weep for me!
In his mercy I am free.
I can neither sow nor spin,
Yet, I am fed and clothed in Him.

I have been the donkey's tail,
Slower than a slug or snail;
You my brothers have been kind,
Never let me lag behind.

I have been most rich in friends,
You have been my feet and hands;
All the good that I could do,
I have done because of you.

Oh my brothers, can't you see?
You have been as Christ for me.
And in my need I know I, too,
Have become as Christ for you!

I have lived for forty years
In this wilderness of tears;
But these trials can't compare
With the glory we will share.

I have had a voice to sing,
To rejoice in everything;
Now Love's sweet eternal song
Breaks the darkness with the dawn.

Brothers do not weep for me!
Christ, the Lord, has set me free.
Oh my friends, remember this:
Pain is not unhappiness.

Growing in Grace & Wisdom

Do you remember when you were a little wiggly kid in Mass? Do you remember when you could barely say the Our Father? What are some spiritual victories you've won—are you more honest, kinder, more forgiving? The purpose behind this project is twofold—first to show you that you have grown and second to encourage you to keep advancing in spiritual growth. We need to reflect on our spiritual progress because we tend to forget and even to become lax. Your parents may mark your physical growth on a growth chart, but your spiritual advances are much more vital.

Usually the sooner you confront a challenge, the easier the challenge will be to solve. Remember, ignoring challenges doesn't make them disappear. Often they become more troublesome because God is trying to get our attention.

Our greatest challenge is getting to Heaven. That is the most important goal and the standard for our creativity and all the rest of our lives. Thanks be to God, we don't have to go it alone. Each person struggling with daily challenges needs to understand that all of Heaven is rooting for him!

Victory Card

Color the image of Our Lady and Jesus on the next page, then remove the page from the book, trim, and fold it in half. Use the lines provided to keep a record of your small but mighty spiritual victories. For example, remembering your morning prayers, paying close attention during Holy Mass, being patient with a younger sibling, obeying right away, using self-control, etc. Each small step toward your goal is a victory to be recorded!

Perhaps you have tried to make progress but have grown discouraged. Maybe you have tried to do too much, too fast. Consider this bit of wisdom: "Life is hard by the yard. By the inch it's a cinch!" For example, if you were to take a bundle of sticks and try to break the whole bundle over your knee, you know you would fail. But, if you were to separate the sticks, you would find it quite easy to break them, one by one. You can do it, one day at a time!

God, grant me the serenity to accept the things I cannot change, the courage to change the things that I can, and the wisdom to know the difference.

"DAY BY DAY LIKE US HE GREW."

12

Creativity is not an end in itself. It is not enough to be creative, just as it is not enough to be clever. If you are clever at lying to others, your cleverness is not doing anyone any real good. Creativity has a purpose. Purposes lead us down specific paths, some of which we may prefer not to go down after rethinking the situation. Let's read about Nina, a girl who needed to rethink the path she was on.

Nina's Trial

"Well, if I can't take St. Teresa of Avila, then I shall not take any saint name at all." Nina Peyton, facing her classmates, brought her small foot down with a very determined stamp.

"Hush, Nina! Please hush!" said Susie Newton. "Sister Rose will hear you!"

"I hope she will!" returned Nina, perversely. "But I don't intend to lose my confirmation name, that's all!"

"Oh, hush!" exclaimed two or three voices together, as the door of the classroom opened and Sister Rose entered.

"What is the matter, children?" she asked, noting at once the air of unusual excitement in the room. "Nina Peyton, why are you out of your seat?"

Nina blushed and gave no answer. There was a naughty, determined expression on her countenance, as she stood there quite still, making no movement toward her seat. Her classmates gazed at her with some apprehension. Surely Nina would not attempt to talk back to Sister Rose!

The nun repeated her question, and now there was something in her voice which compelled obedience.

"Susie Newton says I can't take Teresa for my confirmation name," replied Nina, speaking very fast. "She says six of the girls have already taken Teresa, and that you don't want any more of us to take it. She has no right to boss me, and I will have the name I want, so there!"

"Nina! Nina!" exclaimed Sister Rose. "Is this the spirit of a child preparing for confirmation?"

"I don't care!" continued Nina—but this time there was an odd little catch in her voice. "I want my St. Teresa."

"And why do you want St. Teresa?" she asked, calmly.

Whatever might be her faults, Nina Peyton was a truthful girl, and her answer was somewhat startling.

"Because—because—she was such a great, grand saint. She never did small, little things; she always did the big, grand ones. I plan to do something great and high when I grow up, too. Besides—besides, Susie Newton said I couldn't have her."

"My dear," said Sister Rose, reprovingly, "do you think St. Teresa would wish to be the patron of a girl who chooses her for the reasons you give,

especially the last one? Have you ever read the life of St. Teresa, Nina?"

Nina, in honesty, had to answer, "No." She had, however, read the anecdote of the two little Spanish children—the future saint and her brother—running away from home to seek martyrdom at the hands of the Moors. To Nina's ambitious mind, there was something very enticing in that idea, at least in thought. Since the name of Teresa had not been given her at baptism, she had long hoped to receive it at confirmation. This is why she was so angry and disappointed when she found her wish might not be possible.

Nina had often been heard to declare her intention of becoming a saint herself someday. She would begin on the very next Monday. It would be fine to fight off big sins, and of course, the little ones weren't worth mentioning. She could conquer them without the slightest trouble. Alas, for poor Nina, how many times had she been obliged to make a fresh start! Sometimes an hour of the day had hardly passed before she had "stopped being a saint," as she expressed it. In each case it wasn't a big fault that had caused the fall, but one of those tiny little things which she so despised. She would either lose her temper because she was contradicted, or speak an uncharitable word, or say something unkind to a friend. Then an uncomfortable feeling would come, and Nina felt she would have to begin all over again next Monday. Why she chose Monday was not quite clear even to Nina, except perhaps that the business of a new week began on that day, and one felt fresher and more like making a new start. Even with her repeated beginnings, and the falls always caused by the little things, Nina could not yet see their immense importance. At least she would not see. It is sad to say, she frequently lost her temper over the very thought that those little things could possibly get the better of her again…

"I thought not," said Sister Rose, when Nina acknowledged she had not read the saint's life. "And I do not advise you to read it yet, my dear child," she continued. "It is a wonderful life, which you would not understand till you are older. But I have read it, children," she went on, now addressing the class, "and let me assure you that if St. Teresa did do great things, she did not by any means despise the perfect doing of little things—the very tiny, ordinary things. For the present, be content to do perfectly the little things around you and before you know it, they will be big things."

Sister Rose paused a minute. Some of the girls looked very thoughtful and serious. Nina's expression was one of doubt.

The bell for recess rang. As the girls were filing out, Sister Rose detained Nina for a few moments. Her manner was very kind and gentle as she said: "Nina, if you desire Teresa for your confirmation name you may certainly have it. I did request that the children would not all take the same name, as there are many saints in the calendar; and it sometimes happens that the majority of a class will follow one or two students blindly, like sheep. Susie misunderstood me. You may take whom you choose, provided you are more reverent in future when speaking on such a subject. It is really shocking to think you would quarrel over a saint."

By this time Nina was feeling very repentant and went to the other extreme.

"No, Sister," she said, heroically, "I do not think St. Teresa would want such a person as I am now. I am not worthy. I shall give it up." And Nina had an edified, resigned expression.

"Think it over, dear," answered Sister Rose, smiling a little, "and don't decide too hastily. Remember you have a few weeks yet."

When Nina entered the hall, the girls were talking together very earnestly, but their voices fell to a lower tone as she approached.

"Don't ask her to join; she despises such things," said somebody in a whisper just loud enough for Nina to hear.

"Oh, yes, I will!" replied Susie Newton, who was evidently the ruling spirit. "I wouldn't start up a club without Nina, though we do have little quarrels now and then."

On hearing the remark of the first girl, Nina was about to turn away in high disdain, but Susie's manner and the mention of a club stopped her.

"Want to join the C.L.T. Club?" asked Susie. "It is a secret club, Nina, and it will be such fun! Come on, help make up the rules." And Susie hospitably made room for her on the bench beside her. "You see," she explained, pointing to a paper before her, while a number of eager heads were craned over her shoulder, "C.L.T.C. means Conquer Little Things Club. It just came into my head to start it while Sister Rose was talking. As soon as we get all the rules made up we'll elect a president and design our badges. It will just be so special," continued Susie, becoming more fired up with her idea. "My brothers and all the boys I know belong to clubs, and they're so awfully mysterious about them. How inquisitive they'll be when they see our badges!"

"But go on, Susie, go on with the rules," suggested somebody.

Thus encouraged, Susie began to read from the paper before her. Her tone was very important, as befitting such solemn words:

"Whereas, I hereby vow and resolve on this 20th day of April, in the year of Our Lord 1889, that to the uttermost of my power and ability; whereas, I will comply with the following rules and regulations governing the C.L.T.C.; whereas, resolved, the following rules: Rule one—"

But here somebody interrupted. "My! How could you make it sound so nice and law-ish, Susie?"

"My big brother is going to be a lawyer," announced Susie.

This explanation was enough, and the girls listened with awe at Susie's legal knowledge.

"Go on," said Nina, eagerly. Evidently this was interesting.

"Well, then. Rule One: Don't lose your temper even if people say the smallest, meanest things to you. Rule Two: If people ever make fun of you, don't let them see you care. Rule Three: Don't give a sharp answer, even to the crankiest person in the world. Rule Four: When you feel you are dying for some candy, just conquer your desire and give the money to the poor. Rule Five: Don't insist on people listening to your opinion, give in gently. Rule six: Don't quarrel. Rule Seven: If you have little sisters and brothers, tell them stories when they ask, even when you feel like enjoying a quiet time of reading; and if there's a baby in your family, and you are caring for it, be gentle even when it squeals."

Here Susie paused. "That's all I could think of so far," she said. "Perhaps it's enough. They'll be hard to keep, though they sound easy."

"I don't think so," said Nina, decidedly. "Of course, some of them sound silly enough, but dear me! We can easily do all those things if we make up our minds to it. I think we ought to have a few more rules—really hard ones; there won't be any glory in keeping those tiny things."

"Well, this isn't going to be a club for conquering grand things," replied Susie. "If it proves a success

at the end of the week, then you may make up something of that kind."

Nina reluctantly agreed, and the girls, all very much interested, went about electing a president. Of course, the choice fell upon Susie, who blushingly accepted the honor. Each girl was to make her own badge that evening at home; the badges were to be of white ribbon, embroidered with the mystic letters of the club in gold.

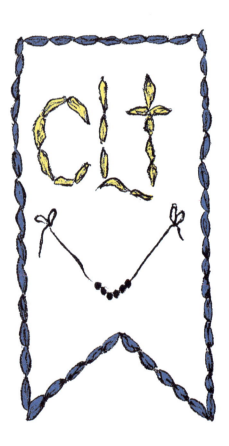

After school that afternoon they went together to a little toyshop, where every girl bought herself a small box containing one hundred common black beads. Each time a member broke one of the rules she was to slip one of these beads on a string. At the end of the week the girl who had the least number on her string was to be crowned with flowers—paper ones would do, Susie explained—and become president the following week. The girl who had strung the greatest number of black beads was to wear a piece of black ribbon over her badge as a sign of disgrace during the following week. And the club was to begin from that very minute, according to the wish of Susie, who, unlike Nina, never thought it necessary to wait until Monday to make a fresh start.

As Nina walked home she entertained two pleasant thoughts: one was that she would probably be the president for the coming week, the other, how very becoming the crown of flowers would be to her. Once or twice however, what Sister Rose had said crossed her mind, and it made her feel slightly uncomfortable. Perhaps Sister Rose had been mistaken, though; and Nina thought she could prove her wrong. By the end of the week, Nina had proven something. Let's follow her home to see what it was.

The girls had copied the rules on separate slips of paper, and our Nina was reading hers over with a scornful smile as she neared home. Suddenly her hat shot swiftly over her eyes; then somehow she was tripping over someone else's foot. And the next instant she found herself sitting on the front door mat—surely a ridiculous position in front of the many people who were passing by on the crowded street. At the same moment, a shout of boyish laughter attested to somebody's enjoyment over the success of his trick. Tommy, the most mischievous of her small brothers, surrounded by three friends of his own size, stood looking at her with amazing glee from the safe position they had taken.

Without an instant's hesitation, her eyes flashing with anger, Nina turned on her brother. Of course, he had anticipated this, and all four made their escape with surprising ease. Nina chased them for a block or more, but at last realized that their head start would not allow her to catch them. Very much ruffled and disordered looking, she returned to the house, vowing she would have Tommy well punished for what he had done.

"Oh Nina, your hair's all coming loose! What's the matter?" asked her sweet little sister on meeting her in the hall.

"Move out of the way, and let me upstairs!" exclaimed Nina crossly.

As she reached the upper landing her mother appeared with the baby in her arms.

"Hold the baby a moment, dear," she said, "I hear your papa calling me." Nina would have refused if she dared. As it was, the poor baby, who was unusually fussy that day, received more impatient shakes in the next three minutes than he ever had before. And as each shake only increased his cries, her mother was sure he was going to have a fit when finally she appeared and claimed him.

Nina darted away to her own room, shut the door and locked it. Then she sat down and tried to spread out the slip of paper, now considerably crumpled, on the small dressing table before her.

"Good gracious, me!" she exclaimed suddenly, as her eyes fell upon the words at the head of the page, "Don't lose your temper…"—"but I've broken a rule already!" Poor Nina almost dropped out of her chair in her amazement. Again her eyes wandered to the paper, and again she read: "Rule Two—and I've broken that, too! But—but how could I help it? Oh, those horrid, horrid boys, to make me break two rules all at once!"

It was very hard, but Nina found courage to go on. She discovered that she had also broken the third—spoken so crossly to her little sister. Then with resignation she decided to find out how many more she had broken.

Rules Four and Five were "all right" she found. "Rule Six: Don't quarrel. Haven't broken that yet," said Nina aloud, "but I will when I catch Tom. I gave the baby a dozen shakes; of course, that means I broke the seventh rule. Oh, dear me! What shall I do?"

The most practical thought that suggested itself was the stringing of her black beads. She took the box out of her pocket, feeling very discouraged indeed, and proceeded to count out five black ones. "Though I only broke four really; still I suppose I'll break that 'Don't quarrel' one," she explained to herself. "But," she added suddenly catching the fifth bead and pulling it off again, "no, I won't. I'll make a fresh start from this minute, I'll let Tom off this time."

Then she proceeded to arrange her hair and dress before appearing downstairs again. She had immense faith in herself still, and certainly, she was not going to lose courage over four black beads.

At the dinner table that evening, Tommy was the last to make his appearance. When he did come in he slipped hastily into his place, glancing from under a pair of twinkling eyes at Nina. But Nina was serene and gracious to an extraordinary degree. Tommy's courage went up like mercury in a thermometer suddenly brought from a cold room into one greatly heated.

"I say, Nina," he began, sidling up to his sister a little later, "want some daisy candy?"

Nina was not by any means above sweets, and accepted Tom's reparation at once.

"Good, isn't it?" said the boy, regarding her with great interest as she tasted the morsel.

"It's delicious!" agreed Nina. "But where did you get it, Tom?"

"In that new store round on the avenue," was the answer. "And, gee, but it's dandy cheap, two pounds for a quarter!"

"Really!" exclaimed the little girl incredulously.

"I wish I had some more," said Nina as she finished the enticing morsel. "I feel so much like enjoying some candy tonight."

"I'll go buy you some," answered her small brother willingly. "Get two pounds, Nina. It's only a quarter, you know."

Nina opened her purse; she had just twenty-five cents remaining of her monthly allowance. A shadow suddenly darkened the dining-room window near which the two were sitting, and a timid knock sounded at the basement door. Cook opened it, muttered, "Be off at once!" and then slammed it quickly again. "Nothing but pestering beggars!" Then two barefoot little boys slowly passed the window again and were lost to sight in the dim street.

"Jane is an old crank. She should have given those poor children something," remarked Nina, indignantly.

"Come on, give me the money," said Tommy, uninterestedly, "it's getting late."

Nina drew it forth—at the same time, her paper with the list of rules fell on the floor. She picked it up quickly, and it then flashed across her mind that she was about to break another rule: "Rule Four: When you feel like you are dying for some candy, just conquer your desire, and give the money to the poor." Two beggars had just appeared, and she had let them go empty-handed.

"Well, but that wasn't my fault," Nina consoled herself. "It was that stingy old Jane's fault. I never thought."

And now that the beggars were really gone, Tommy might as well get the candy; it wasn't likely any others would come that night. And he did get the candy, the wonderful candy that was going for such a bargain. Nina consoled herself by sharing it generously with all the children, though the consequences proved rather disastrous; for Mother was up nearly all night administering medicine to the younger ones who had eaten too much of it.

Poor Nina herself felt wretched the following morning. She sat in the classroom feeling very miserable and dejected, partly the effect of the candy and the dose of medicine, and partly from the knowledge that her string held the largest number of black beads. She had broken the rules seven times the evening before, and four times again before starting for school that morning. Nina was five black beads ahead of any other member of the Club.

For the first time, it began to dawn upon Nina that she had allowed the little things to conquer her all her life. The truth was a very unpleasant one, and yet it was staring her in the face. Nina, knowing she had more beads than the others, felt herself growing to be a very humbled, heartbroken little girl. On the morning of the fifth day her box was empty, her string was full. Then she broke down altogether.

"Never mind, Nina," said Susie Newton, with her arms tightly clasped around her, while the others looked on compassionately. "We know it's harder for you because you never could see the use of thinking of the little things."

"But I tried very, very hard this week," sobbed Nina. "I didn't ever think I'd try so hard with little things, and now it hasn't been a bit of use."

"Yes, it has," said Sister Rose, who had broken in upon the group, and to whom the secret of the Club had, of course, been confided. "Poor child," she continued, softly stroking Nina's hair, "it has taught you golden lessons in humility, and the folly of trusting to your own strength even in conquering those troublesome little things. My Nina is a much better child today than she was a week ago."

"I never felt more wicked in my life, Sister," said Nina, lifting a very tear-stained face. "I don't think there's a worse person in the world. It doesn't seem any use to try anymore." Nina did look very dejected.

"Courage, Nina, courage!" said Sister brightly. "Try again and don't lose heart even if you do fail. It is much harder to be patient with ourselves than to be so with others."

Two weeks later Nina took her place in the procession of white-veiled girls about to be confirmed. Her card bore the name of Teresa. Sister Rose had insisted upon that. But it was a trembling, contrite, and humble little heart that Nina offered to her great patron.

Conquer Little Things

My God, I have never thanked Thee for my thorn. I have thanked Thee a thousand times for my roses, but not once for my thorn. —George Matheson

Each person has some particular thorn in the side. We are all prone to at least one strong temptation. This temptation is an opportunity to grow in grace. If you know that you are prone to talking back or laziness, think ahead and make preparations to defeat these attitudes or to steer clear of them. Denial of our weakness is not wise. We make or unmake ourselves each day.

Invite family members to join you in "conquering little things." With your own money, buy a big bag of wrapped tootsie-roll pops. Place a short glass jar or large-mouthed vase on your family's prayer table. Cut out the label below and paste it on the jar. When a family member has made a good effort to conquer a bad habit, he can place a tootsie pop upright in the jar like a flower. Be sure to pray for each other!

Once the jar is full of colorful pops, come together to decide what you will do with the colorful bouquet to celebrate conquering little things. Ideas could include watching a family movie as you enjoy the pops, bringing the pops along on a Sunday picnic, or gifting the bouquet to the firemen at your local fire station or the volunteers at your local pro-life center.

SMALL THINGS WITH GREAT LOVE
—ST. THERESE

13

Friendship is an important area for us to use creativity. Our creativity should be used for good, to help others. Using our gift of creativity is often a choice we make. Let's read a story about two friends who chose to respond creatively to the challenges they faced.

Damon and Pythias

A young man whose name was Pythias had done something which the tyrant Dionysius did not like. For this offense he was dragged to prison, and a day was set when he should be put to death. His home was far away, and he wanted very much to see his father and mother and friends before he died.

"Only give me leave to go home and say good-bye to those whom I love," he said, "and then I will come back and give up my life."

The tyrant laughed at him.

"How can I know that you will keep your promise?" he said. "You only want to cheat me, and save yourself."

Then a young man whose name was Damon spoke and said,—

"O king! put me in prison in place of my friend Pythias, and let him go to his own country to put his affairs in order, and to bid his friends farewell. I know that he will come back as he promised, for he is a man who has never broken his word. But if he is not here on the day which you have set, then I will die in his stead."

The tyrant was surprised that anybody should make such an offer. He at last agreed to let Pythias go, and gave orders that the young man Damon should be shut up in prison.

Time passed, and by and by the day drew near which had been set for Pythias to die; and he had not come back. The tyrant ordered the jailer to keep close watch upon Damon, and not let him escape. But Damon did not try to escape. He still had faith in the truth and honor of his friend. He said, "If Pythias does not come back in time, it will not be his fault. It will be because he is hindered against his will."

At last the day came, and then the very hour. Damon was ready to die. His trust in his friend was as firm as ever; and he said that he did not grieve at having to suffer for one whom he loved so much.

Then the jailer came to lead him to his death; but at the same moment Pythias stood in the door. He had been delayed by storms and shipwreck, and he had feared that he was too late. He greeted Damon kindly, and then gave himself into the hands of the jailer. He was happy because he had come in time, even though it was at the last moment.

The tyrant was not so bad but that he could see good in others. He felt that men who loved and trusted each other, as did Damon and Pythias, ought to be spared. And so he set them both free.

"I would give all my wealth to have one such friend," he said.

Translated from the Greek by James Baldwin

**"Greater love has no man than this,
that a man lay down his life for his friends."** (John 15:13)

What It Takes to Be a Good Friend

Refer to this list often, especially before getting together with a friend!

- I seldom brag about the things I've done or the things I have.

- I am a good listener. When someone is talking to me, I show that I am interested by paying close attention to what he is saying.

- I seldom lose my temper, even when another person speaks in a mean way to me, or even when things go wrong for me.

- Remembering my own mistakes, I try not to criticize the mistakes of others.

- Even when things are not just the way I want them to be, I try not to complain or find fault.

- I try to be charitable in speech, and to not talk about the faults of others.

- I do not try to think up excuses for my mistakes, and I do not resent it if someone tries to show me how to do something a better way.

- I am grateful and say "thank you" often.

- I am quick to apologize if I have accidentally hurt or offended someone.

- I do not show off.

- When there is a job to be done, I can be counted on to do my share of the work.

- I am quick to offer my help to anyone I am able to help.

- I am generous and always willing to share my time and things with others.

- I do not try to lie my way out of tight spots. I tell the truth and take the consequences.

- I have a good reputation for being honest and truthful.

- If something is told to me in confidence, I don't pass it around—not even to my best friend.

What It Takes to Be a Big Nuisance

This formula is guaranteed to make you miserable.

- Think about yourself.
- Talk about yourself.
- Use "I" as often as possible.
- Expect to be appreciated.
- Be suspicious, jealous, and envious.
- Be sensitive to the slightest negative comment.
- Never forget a criticism.
- Trust nobody but yourself.
- Love yourself supremely.

- Demand full agreement with your opinions on everything.
- Sulk and pout if others are not grateful for your attention and help.
- Keep reminding people of the help you have given them.
- Be on the lookout for a good time for yourself.
- Shirk your chores and duties whenever you can get away with it.
- Be selfish.

14

As you continue to cultivate creativity within yourself, keep mature creativity as your goal. Creativity is at its best when it is truly visionary, truly resourceful, truly responsible, and truly loving. Thanks to an unusual dream, the boy in this story "wakes up" to the need to use his abilities in a loving and mature way.

Alfred Has a Dream

"Well, Alfred," I said, "I'm glad to see you took my little talk to heart. I've noticed quite a difference in you these last few days."

Our Knights of the Altar meeting had just broken up. I had a chance to speak to Alfred because he was the last one to leave.

"What talk?" he asked.

His question sort of took the wind out of my sails. Just the week before I had given the altar boys a nice little talk. At least I thought it was a nice little talk. I had explained that it was important for an altar boy to do a good job of serving. But I also said that it was even more important to have our minds on the Mass, and to be thinking of Jesus as we serve Him.

"If I had to choose," I had told the servers, "between an altar boy who can serve perfectly but doesn't love the Mass, and an altar boy who makes a few mistakes but does love Jesus in the Mass—then I'd surely take the altar boy who makes the mistakes."

To tell the truth, I was aiming my talk mostly at Alfred. He was a good server, sharp and quick. But he was just a little too proud of his serving.

If his fellow altar server at Mass was a little slow, Alfred would hiss at him like a snake, or snap his fingers like a firecracker. If the other boy made a mistake, Alfred would look awfully disgusted and would go, "tsk, tsk." He was so bossy and know-it-all around the sacristy, that he was getting pretty unpopular with the other Knights of the Altar.

The first couple of days after my talk Alfred was just the same as usual. (He was serving my eight o'clock Mass that week.) Then suddenly overnight there was a big change. No more finger-snapping or hissing or bossing. Just a good altar boy minding his own business—and God's business. So I thought my talk had finally sunk in. That is what I meant when I told Alfred that I had noticed a big change in him.

"What talk, Father?" Alfred had answered. Then he went on. "I don't remember any talk, but I sure had a dream the other night. I dreamed that I died and went to Heaven. Tony Martelli was right ahead of me." (Tony is another one of our altar servers.)

"I saw St. Peter smile at Tony and shake hands with him. Then the big gates swung open and Tony walked in. The gates were just like those

103

at the ball park, only these were gold. The gates started to swing shut again, so I began to run to catch up with Tony before the gates closed. But St. Peter grabbed me by the collar as I was going by. He said, 'Not so fast, young fellow. You're not going in there for a while yet. You've got some homework to do first.'

"That made me kind of mad. 'Why not?' I asked St. Peter. 'If Tony got in I ought to get in. I served more Masses than he did. And I served better, too.'

"Then St. Peter pulled a little book out of his pocket. 'It says in here,' St. Peter told me, 'that Tony Martelli loves to serve Mass so that he can be close to Jesus. It says that sometimes Tony is thinking so much about Jesus or praying so hard that he forgets to ring the bell.

"Then St. Peter turned a page in the book. 'It also says in here,' St. Peter told me, 'that Alfred Hicks loves to serve Mass because he likes people to see how smart he is. He is very proud of himself. At Mass he is thinking more about himself than he is thinking about Jesus.'

"Then St. Peter snapped the rubber band around the book, and put it back in his pocket. I was pretty scared by that time. 'Alfred,' he said, 'I'll be seeing you again later. But first I've got to send you down to get some of that pride out of you.'

"St. Peter reached over to the wall and pushed a button. Suddenly the ground dropped away from under my feet. I was shooting down a long dark tunnel that smelled like our basement when Mom's doing her laundry on Monday morning. Right then I woke up, and gee was I glad! Mom was shaking me and telling me to hurry or I'd be late for Mass."

Alfred was silent for a second or two. "Of course it was only a dream," he said, "but it made me think … Father, what was that you said about a talk?"

"Never mind, Alfred," I answered. "I think you know all about it anyway."

Adapted from a story written by Rev. Leo Trese

Donkeys or Saints?

What we find entertaining, enjoyable, and amusing depends on the states of mind that we develop and become accustomed to. What we consider to be fun may in reality be either harmful or good for us. In the story of Pinocchio, the boys who devote themselves to false pleasures in the Land of Toys (or Pleasure Island) gradually change into donkeys. This applies to us, too, because what we enjoy changes who we are. What will our fun turn us into? Do we wish to be donkeys or saints?

Try seeing your fun time as a chance to grow as a person. For instance, good movies and books are not only enjoyable, they are also opportunities to think more deeply about the characters' decisions and about the artistic skill shown by the author or movie producer.

The projects below are examples of how you can turn your fun time into productive entertainment, or how you can make a task you dislike more enjoyable. Over the next few days or weeks, complete at least three of these projects.

☐ After watching a good movie or reading a book together have a casual family discussion. Some questions for books or movies: Who was your favorite character? What did you like best about that character? Do any of the characters remind you of someone you know either in another story or in real life? Did you like the opening? Would you have written the ending differently? What are some of the virtues shown? Which characters are motivated by fear, ambition, or anger? Think of another title for the movie or book.

☐ Watch a movie for a second time and focus on a particular aspect. Try paying attention to the music, the scenery, minor characters, special effects, close-up shots and other camera angles, and the results of a character's decisions.

☐ Review a movie or book using prudence as a guideline. Who was prudent and who was not? How did the wise characters show their prudence? Did fear control any of the characters and destroy their prudence? What was the result?

☐ Think of a chore you don't like doing, but that has to be done anyway. Now think of a way to make it more enjoyable or at least bearable. Would listening to music help? How about offering the chore up for someone who is having a hard time? Some chores could be done with your left hand if you are right-handed, or you could time yourself to see how long the chore actually takes.

15

God gave us bodies to stretch, minds for wondering, trees for climbing, hands for holding, voices for laughing, and hearts for caring. Entertainment has an impact on who we are becoming and on our relationships with each other. That's why good sportsmanship is important. Good sportsmanship recognizes that sports are also about relationships. Let's read about a group of boys who truly practiced good sportsmanship.

The Baseball Game

At a fund-raising dinner for a school that serves learning disabled children, the father of one of the students delivered a speech that would never be forgotten by any who attended. After extolling the school and its dedicated staff, he offered a question.

"When not interfered with by outside influences, everything nature does is done with perfection. Yet my son, Shay, cannot learn things as other children do. He cannot understand things as other children do. Where is the natural order of things in my son?"

The audience was stilled by the query.

The father continued. "I believe, that when a child like Shay comes into the world, an opportunity to realize true human nature presents itself, and it comes in the way other people treat that child."

Then he told the following story:

Shay and his father had walked past a park where some boys Shay knew were playing baseball.

Shay asked, "Do you think they'll let me play?"

Shay's father knew that most of the boys would not want someone like Shay on their team, but the father also understood that if his son were allowed to play, it would give him a much-needed sense of belonging.

Shay's father approached one of the boys on the field and asked if Shay could play. The boy looked around for guidance and, getting none, he took matters into his own hands and said, "We're losing by six runs, and the game is in the eighth inning. I guess he can be on our team, and we'll try to put him in to bat in the ninth inning."

In the bottom of the eighth inning, Shay's team scored a few runs but was still behind by three. In the top of the ninth inning, Shay put on a glove and played in the outfield.

Even though no hits came his way, he was obviously ecstatic just to be in the game and on the field, grinning from ear to ear as his father waved to him from the stands.

In the bottom of the ninth inning, Shay's team scored again. Now, with two outs and the bases loaded, the potential winning run was on base, and Shay was scheduled to be next at bat.

At this juncture, would they let Shay bat and give away their chance to win the game?

Surprisingly, Shay was given the bat. Everyone knew that a hit was all but impossible. Shay didn't even know how to hold the bat properly, much less connect with the ball.

However, as Shay stepped up to the plate, the pitcher moved in a few steps to lob the ball in softly so Shay could at least be able to make contact.

The first pitch came, and Shay swung clumsily and missed. The pitcher again took a few steps forward to toss the ball softly toward Shay. As the pitch came in, Shay swung at the ball and hit a slow ground ball right back to the pitcher.

The pitcher picked up the soft grounder and could have easily thrown the ball to the first baseman. Shay would have been out and that would have been the end of the game.

Instead, the pitcher took the ball and turned and threw the ball on a high arc to right field, far beyond the reach of the first baseman.

Everyone started yelling, "Shay, run to first! Run to first!"

Never in his life had Shay ever made it to first base. He scampered down the baseline, wide-eyed and startled.

Everyone yelled, "Run to second, run to second!"

By the time Shay rounded first base, the right fielder had the ball. He could have thrown the ball to the second-baseman for the tag, but he understood the pitcher's intentions and intentionally threw the ball high and far over the third-baseman's head.

Shay ran toward second base as the runners ahead of him deliriously circled the bases toward home. Shay reached second base. The opposing short-stop ran to him, turned him in the direction of third base, and shouted, "Run to third!"

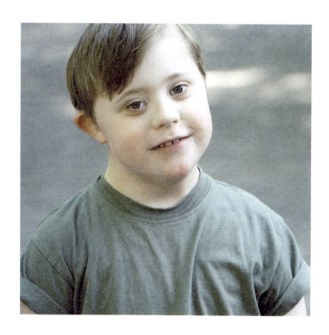

As Shay rounded third, the boys from both teams were screaming, "Shay, run home!" Shay ran to home, stepped on the plate, and was cheered as the hero who hit the "grand slam" and won the game for his team.

"That day," said the father softly with tears now rolling down his face, "the boys from both teams helped bring a piece of true love and humanity into this world."

Playing the Game

Play can be a way to become comfortable with something strange or someone new. Chefs "play" with new combinations of spices and different techniques for garnishing dishes. Our work and our play can be refreshing for others and us. Imagine Jesus and St. Joseph working on something in their shop. Can you see them creating with a sense of pleasure at the thought of making something worthwhile for another person?

Because we are created in the image of God, even our entertainment must have limits. To step outside the limits of love is not amusing or creative, but destructive. Games without rules are unplayable. If you could score in basketball without using the basket, the game wouldn't be basketball. Over the next few days, complete at least three of the following activities to practice positive creativity.

☐ Play a game without any props. Have you tried Charades? Sing several rounds of "Row, Row, Row Your Boat" or "Frere Jacques" ("Are You Sleeping?"). Can you harmonize? Can you tell interesting stories to each other? These can be real stories or made up stories or stories about what you would like to do one day.

☐ Does your family enjoy watching and reading mysteries and trying to figure out the endings? Try taking turns reading one sentence out of some of your favorite books. The other players try to guess the title of the book.

☐ Turn a competitive game into a cooperative game. Try building your own obstacle course together. Then complete the course while holding hands.

☐ Build an edible edifice out of various cookies, graham crackers, marshmallows, chocolate bars, and creamy peanut butter. Use the peanut butter as glue. Then eat it.

16

Set aside time to be quiet and pray creatively. We pray creatively when we consider with loving care our relationship with God. If you are praying and you aren't changing into a better person, then your prayer is not creative. Prayer is one of the most effective ways of changing our world and ourselves. Let's read a story about a girl whose daily prayer made her a willing cooperater in God's plan.

The Friend of the Queen

by Elaine Woodfield

It was a very cold morning as Bernadette Soubirous put on her socks and shoes. When she was done, she took her rosary from the table and put it in the pocket of her skirt; she never went anywhere without it. She shivered in the cold room. Her family needed more firewood but was too poor to buy any, so Bernadette and her sister volunteered to collect driftwood from the bank of the river that flowed just outside of their hometown of Lourdes, in the rocky mountains of southern France.

The family was very poor, so poor that they lived in a damp building that used to be the town jail and had been deserted until they came to live there. Bernadette suffered from asthma, which is a difficulty in breathing, from living in the cold and damp.

If Bernadette could see into the future on that cold morning of February 11, 1858, she would see unbelievable sights. She would see her little neighbor, Louis-Justin Bouhohorts, who was always very sick and was completely paralyzed; he had never walked, even though he was a year and a half old. He would become so sick that

he would be expected to live only a few hours more, when his mother would take him to a new, clean spring of water and bathe him there, full of faith in the goodness of Our Lady, the Blessed Virgin Mary. She would take him home, and he would sleep the whole night through and in the morning, he would rise and walk! And the most amazing thing of all was that this complete cure would come about because of Bernadette herself!

If Bernadette could see even further into the future, she would see a beautiful new church, and thousands upon thousands of people coming to Lourdes. Many hopelessly sick people would be completely cured, and all who came would return home with a deep, wonderful peace in their hearts. All of this would happen because of Bernadette and her loving obedience to Our Lady!

Bernadette could not see into the future, of course! All she knew that morning was that her asthma was acting up. She and her sister walked to the river, and on the way, Bernadette worried that nearness to the river would bring on another attack. But her family needed wood, and

Bernadette's love for them always came first. A friend joined them, and the three girls walked on.

They came to the Grotto, a rough wall of rock arched a little like a cave, which stood beside the river. Bernadette's sister saw some driftwood on the other bank of the river. She removed her shoes and socks and waded across; the other girl followed her. Bernadette hesitated, then stooped to remove her shoes. She watched her sister reach the other bank and collect an armful of wood.

All of a sudden, she heard a sound like a strong wind. Then she saw a golden cloud appear near the Grotto. Within this light, there appeared a beautiful lady! We will let Bernadette herself tell us what happened next.

"She looked at me immediately, smiled at me, and motioned me to come closer, as if she had been my mother; all fear left me. I seemed to know no longer where I was. I rubbed my eyes; I shut them; I opened them. But the Lady was still there, continuing to smile at me and making me understand that I was not mistaken. Without thinking of what I was doing, I took my rosary in my hands and went to my knees. The Lady made a sign of approval with her head and took into her hands her own rosary which hung on her right arm."

While Bernadette prayed each Hail Mary, the Lady let her rosary beads glide silently through her fingers one by one, but she did join Bernadette in saying the Glory Be's.

After the Rosary was completed, the Lady smiled and disappeared. Who was she?

Bernadette's sister and her friend did not see anyone. But Bernadette knew that she would never forget the beautiful Lady in blue and white.

"She is so beautiful that to see her once again, one would be willing to die," Bernadette said many years later, remembering this day.

Later that evening, the family gathered around the warm fireplace. As Bernadette stared into the merry fire, she was remembering the Lady. With all her heart she wanted to see her again. She wondered if the Lady could be the Blessed Virgin. But why would she appear to Bernadette?

As we know, Bernadette was very poor. She had very little schooling, because in those days only the children of the wealthy were educated. But Bernadette was humble and loving. A few years before, a friend of Bernadette's mother offered to take care of Bernadette on her large farm. The woman was wealthy, and promised that Bernadette would receive an education and learn her catechism. The woman gave her only a few catechism lessons, and then sent her to look after her sheep!

Did Bernadette become angry or upset? It would not be amazing at all if she did. But the most amazing thing of all was that Bernadette did not get angry with the woman! She knew that Our Lady never holds a grudge against anyone who wrongs her; rather, she always prays for them. Bernadette did the same. She said her Rosary many times each day under the bright sky as she tended the sheep that she loved. She was happy for the two years she tended sheep. When she finally returned to her family, saying the Rosary was Bernadette's most beloved habit. In her purity and love, Bernadette resembled Our Lady, and this pleased God very much. Perhaps this is why God sent the Lady to appear to Bernadette.

Soon after, Bernadette hurried to the Grotto, and again the Lady appeared and said the Rosary with Bernadette. On February 18th, the Lady appeared again at the Grotto. Only Bernadette saw her, but word had spread through the town and many people knelt behind Bernadette and said the Rosary when she did. The Lady was as beautiful as ever. She leaned toward Bernadette, as one friend will lean toward another to confide some news.

"Will you do me the kindness of coming here every day for two weeks?" asked the Lady.

Bernadette caught her breath. The Lady was asking her for a favor? What a gracious way to ask!

"Yes! Yes, I will!" Bernadette whispered.

The Lady smiled, and then she spoke.

"I do not promise to make you happy in this world but in the next." Bernadette paused to take in the meaning of what the Lady said, then nodded. She accepted with all her heart.

The Lady appeared many times to Bernadette at the Grotto—nineteen times in all! She asked Bernadette many times, "Pray for sinners!" One time, people who knelt near Bernadette saw her face change. Usually she had a beautiful smile on her face when she was seeing the Lady, but this time her face grew very sad. Then she turned to the people and said, "Penitence! Penitence!"

The Lady had told her that God wishes people to stop sinning and do penance in order to appease the just anger of God. Unrepented sins draw down all sorts of misfortune on mankind, and souls who die without repenting of their mortal sins cast themselves into Hell. When a person does penance, he or she helps to draw blessings down on all people, and many accept the grace to return to God's friendship. This was a turning point in Bernadette's life. She bore all her sufferings patiently and offered them as a holy penance to God. In this way, Bernadette found sweetness within suffering all her life long!

The Lady appeared again and again. Then came the Day of the Spring.

"Drink from the spring," directed the Lady.

What spring? Bernadette wondered what the Lady could mean. Perhaps she was referring to the river. She walked toward it. The Lady called her back, pointed to a spot on the ground, and told her to dig there. Using her hands and a stick, Bernadette dug the soil.

All of a sudden, the ground became moist, then wet. A spring started to flow! Bernadette drank the water. Later, a man who had been blind for 20 years washed his eyes with water from the spring that was brought to him. The next day, he could see perfectly! Word spread around the town like wildfire. Mrs. Bouhohorts heard about the spring, and took her sick child Louis-Justin there. We know what happened next!

The Lady asked that a chapel be built at the Grotto. On March 25th, Bernadette had a strong desire to ask the Lady her name. Her parish priest had also asked this of Bernadette. She asked the Lady twice and received no answer but a smile. Then she asked a third time, and we'll let Bernadette tell us what happened next.

"The Lady was standing above the rosebush in a position similar to that shown on the Miraculous Medal," said Bernadette. "At my third request, her face became very serious, and she seemed to

Photo of Bernadette Soubirous

bow down in an attitude of humility. Then she joined her hands and raised them to her breast. She looked up to heaven. Then slowly opening her hands and leaning toward me, she said to me in a voice vibrating with emotion: 'I am the Immaculate Conception.'"

Bernadette did not know what these words meant. She repeated them over and over as she walked quickly to the parish rectory.

"Did the Lady tell you her name?" asked Fr. Peyramale. He had been skeptical of the apparitions.

"Yes, Father. But I don't understand what she said."

"What did she say, child?"

"She said, 'I am the Immaculate Conception,' Father."

Fr. Peyramale gasped. Then he knew. It must be

true. Bernadette could not possibly "make up" this name!

What is the Immaculate Conception?

It means that from the first instant of her life before she was born, Our Lady was completely free of original sin, since she was destined to be the Mother of Jesus. We know that it is only Jesus' death on the cross that redeems us from our sins. It is as if Jesus' redemptive death on the cross reached back in time to free Mary from ever having the stain of original sin! Mary was always God's friend. This is why her prayers are so powerful. The name "Immaculate Conception" also describes the inseparable unity between Our Lady and the Holy Spirit. St. Maximilian Kolbe meditated on this his whole life long, and he tells us that the action of the Holy Spirit, the Sanctifier (he-who-makes-holy), is always united to that of Mary, our Blessed Mother!

Bernadette learned this and all of her catechism, later. But the day came that Our Lady appeared once again, and then no more. By this time, people all over France were flocking to Lourdes. Officials of the town remained skeptical, and questioned and threatened Bernadette. They put up a fence so that people could not go to the Grotto. But they still came, and stood at a distance, praying to God through Our Lady. The Emperor of France heard about the fence. A family member had been cured by Lourdes water, and so the Emperor himself ordered that the fence come down!

We are nearing the end of our story. What happened to Bernadette?

She made her First Communion that year, at age fourteen. She said it was just as wonderful an experience as seeing Our Lady! She went to school as a charity student, then joined the religious order of nuns who had taught and loved her, the Sisters of Charity. Bernadette's father found a job as a miller grinding grain into flour, and her brothers and sisters grew up, worked, and married.

As a Sister, Bernadette took care of the sick in the infirmary. The saint who was responsible for bringing God's healing to so many was never to be healed herself. Her asthma got worse and she developed tuberculosis, an often fatal disease that begins in the lungs. But she was always cheerful and patient. She joked that it was her job to be ill. Bernadette knew that bearing with sufferings and offering them as a penance to God was a wonderful way to serve Him.

Bernadette had a gift for telling funny stories and singing songs. She loved all the children who came with their parents to the convent to visit.

Dozens and dozens of people asked Bernadette about Our Lady's visits, asking the same questions over and over. Bernadette never once lost her patience! The Church approved the visits as authentic, and a beautiful church was built at the Grotto. The water of the spring was channeled so that the sick can be easily bathed in it. Many people are also cured during the procession of the Blessed Eucharist.

But not Bernadette. She died of tuberculosis at age thirty-five, praying, "Holy Mary, Mother of God, pray for me, a poor sinner."

Although she died in 1879, Bernadette's body remains incorrupt. She lies in her convent chapel behind glass, an indescribably beautiful young woman who looks as if she is asleep. She was canonized a saint of the Catholic Church in 1933. Guess who was present in Rome that day to witness the pope proclaim Bernadette a saint? Louis-Justin Bouhohorts, a healthy, vigorous man in his seventies!

Mary is our model of obedience to God's will. To practice what God wants, instead of what we want, use the picture of the Annunciation below to help you. Color a part of the scene any time you put the needs of others before your own wants. For example, when your mother calls you to set the table for supper or to take out the trash, stop what you are doing and go about the chore with a joyful attitude. Soon you will have a colorful masterpiece to remind you of the joy of saying YES to God.

"Behold the handmaid of the Lord: be it done to me according to thy word." (Luke 1:38)

17

As Catholics, we have two thousand years of heritage to draw upon. Our treasury is deep and rich. We have a wealth of devotions, scholarship, books, magazines, saints, prayers, artwork, music, architecture, and true guidance at our disposal. Our Catholic Faith frees us to live fruitfully in the present time. In fact, we must be fruitful wherever we find ourselves. God commands us to bear good fruit. In every age that command required creativity from His sincere disciples. Let's read a story about a saint that lived his Catholic Faith and bore good fruit during a difficult time in history.

Love Alone Creates

by Elaine Woodfield

About eighty years ago, during World War II, millions of men, women, and children suffered and died in terrible places called concentration camps. A man named Adolph Hitler ruled Germany and had conquered most of Europe with his skilled armies, and it was he who was responsible for these camps. He and his followers, called Nazis, were atheistic, which means that they did not believe in God and hated all people who did. They also were totalitarian, which means that they believed that their way of governing the people was "the perfect way," and that they had a right to terrorize and kill anyone who opposed them in the slightest. They also believed that some people were deserving of death just because of who they were, such as Jews, gypsies, priests, slaves, and weak, ill, or handicapped persons.

Such persons were arrested, crammed aboard freight trains for days without food, and taken to the camps. Their luggage was taken away, and they were given a striped uniform and hard wooden shoes. The prisoners were forced to work for thirteen or more hours a day. They had nothing to eat each day except a few crusts of stale bread and some weak soup, and they were mistreated by cruel guards for little or no reason. The prisoners

lived in crowded, unheated bunk houses, grouped together in "blocks." They became very thin, tired, and sick, and one by one they died. Those who got off the train looking weak or ill were sent to be killed almost right away.

One of these places was called Auschwitz, in Poland. There were many such camps in Europe during World War II, and millions of people died. A place like Auschwitz truly was terrible, wasn't it? But even in a place like this, God's glory can shine brightly in the love and faith of His saints. They remembered that Jesus was cruelly mistreated and unjustly killed, and imitated Him in His patience, forgiveness, and love. One of many saints to live and die in the camps was Fr. Maximilian Kolbe. His heroic story shows us that belonging to God through consecration to our Blessed Mother can help us walk securely—even fly—to God on our lifelong journey to His kingdom.

Life in the camps was awful indeed. But never was Fr. Kolbe heard to complain. He regularly gave up his small ration of bread to the sick, and he prayed with people. He secretly heard the confessions of those who were dying, although this was strictly forbidden and punishable by death. But Fr. Kolbe would gladly risk his own life to bring the Sacrament of Confession to any prisoner. He gave conferences to his fellow prisoners, speaking to them about how much God and Our Lady loved and cared for them. The prisoners were greatly comforted by these conferences, and eagerly gathered around Fr. Kolbe to hear his words, even though they were risking punishment to do so.

The Nazis especially hated priests, and several times Nazi guards would beat Fr. Kolbe mercilessly for no reason. Fr. Kolbe was often heard to say, "For Jesus Christ I am prepared to suffer still more." He knew that all suffering offered gladly to God is a precious prayer that can bring many blessings to souls.

Fr. Kolbe suffered most of his life from tuberculosis, and life in the concentration camp made it get much worse. His breathing became difficult and painful. When he visited the infirmary for medical treatment, he often gave his place in the infirmary hospital to another, and gave food to and prayed with those who were very sick. This amazed the camp doctors.

One prisoner remembered him saying, "Hate is not creative. Our sorrow is necessary that those who live after us may be happy."

Another time, he said, "No, they will not kill our souls. They will not be able to deprive us of the dignity of being a Catholic. We will not give up and when we die, then we die pure and peaceful, resigned to God in our hearts."

One day a prisoner from Block 14, which was Fr. Kolbe's block, was found missing at evening roll call. He had escaped! While guards and dogs searched for him, all of the prisoners of Block 14 had to stand rigidly at attention in the sun for hours while Fritsch, the camp Kommandant, paced back and forth before them. The men were very tired and hungry. At last, soup was brought, and the hungry men's mouths watered at the delicious smell. Then Fritsch ordered that the soup be dumped down the drain in front of them!

No one slept much that night. Each man was wondering if he would be one of the ten prisoners selected at random to be placed in "The Bunker" to be starved to death in retaliation for the one prisoner's escape. Unfair? You bet it was. But the Nazis knew that this rule would make any prisoner think twice about escaping if he knew that ten men he left behind in the camp would be put to death because of his escape.

The men of Block 14 lined up for morning roll call. Fritsch kept them standing straight at attention in the hot July sun without food all day long! By evening roll call, the escaped prisoner had not been found. Fritsch walked among the lines of men slowly picking ten men at random. Gasps of horror were heard along with sighs of relief. One man who was chosen to die, Sergeant Francis Gajowniczek, wept aloud, saying, "What will become of my wife and children?"

One of the prisoners stepped out of line and calmly walked up to Kommandant Fritsch, and respectfully removed his hat. Everyone was

shocked! No one was allowed to step out of line or even speak without permission — the guards were ordered to shoot anyone who did so immediately. But even the guards were too surprised to do anything but stare. Perhaps a heavenly Lady had them pause at the importance of what happened next.

Fritsch scowled at the prisoner, "What does this Polish pig want?" The prisoner stood calm and smiling.

"I would like to die in the place of this man," said the prisoner, pointing to Sergeant Gajowniczek.

"Why?" barked Fritsch.

"Because he has a wife and children. I am an old, sick man, of no use to anyone." The prisoner knew what to say in order to have Fritsch agree with his request, because the Nazis thought that the sick and weak were not worth keeping alive.

"And who are you?" shouted Fritsch.

"A Catholic priest," said the prisoner calmly.

The prisoners strained to see who this prisoner was. It was Fr. Maximilian Kolbe!

Everyone held their breaths.

What would Kommandant Fritsch do? wondered each man.

Fritsch might order the priest executed immediately, or might throw both the sergeant and the priest in the Bunker.

"Request accepted!" he ordered. So Fr. Kolbe's number of 16670 was added to the list, and the sergeant's was removed.

All present were still amazed at what they had just witnessed. For never had it happened in the terrible camp of Auschwitz, in the memory of any prisoner or guard, that anyone had offered his own life to preserve the life of another prisoner!

The sun was setting as the ten prisoners were led away to the Bunker. Those who survived the camp remembered that particular sunset all of their lives, because it was so brilliant and such a bright, beautiful red sky. It was Fr. Kolbe's last sight of the outside world, and he knew that it was a loving message from Our Lady, whom he always called the Immaculata. She was reminding him of something that happened long ago, and telling him that his sacrifice was accepted.

Photo of Fr. Maximilian Kolbe

But who was Fr. Maximilian Kolbe? Where did he come from? Why was he especially close to Our Lady, the Immaculata? And what kind of life did he live that would result in him "laying down his life for his friend"?

Fr. Kolbe was born on January 8, 1894 in Zdunka-Wola, a small Polish town on the outskirts of Lodz, a large industrial city.

His name was Raymond, and he was the second of three sons. The Kolbe family obtained raw materials weekly from Lodz, and worked long hours each week weaving cloth out of them. The pay was meager, and the family was poor. As the boys grew, the family was able to better itself; Mrs. Kolbe opened a small secondhand store and Mr. Kolbe grew vegetables in several garden plots. The family was very devoted to God. A picture of Our Lady of Jasna Gora, the Queen of Poland, hung in a place of honor wherever they lived, and young Raymond passed many happy times gazing at Our Lady and pouring his heart out to her in prayer.

Raymond could be mischievous, and punishment in the Kolbe household was quickly administered by a switch. Raymond always submitted to his punishment, knowing that it was just.

After one incident of misbehavior and punishment, Mrs. Kolbe, her heart breaking, said to Raymond, "Tell me, my son, what is ever going to become of you?"

The words seemed to embed themselves in Raymond's heart. He could not forget them. "What will become of me? What will become of me?" he asked himself over and over. He knew that the answer to that question lay in what he did now, as a child. And how to change himself? How to become better? That was very hard. What to do?

He went to his parish church, knelt down before the altar of Our Lady, and poured his heart out to her. He asked her to help him leave behind his disobedient ways, and he prayed much before her picture at home, too. Raymond was not afraid to cry as he asked Our Lady to show him what would happen to him. One day while he was praying in church, a wonderful thing happened. Our Lady appeared to him in breathtaking beauty. She smiled, and offered him two crowns. One was white, meaning that he would always be chaste and pure, and the other crown was red, meaning that he would give up his life for God and die a martyr's death.

Our Lady looked lovingly at Raymond, and asked him which of the two crowns he wanted.

"I would like both," he said.

Our Lady gazed lovingly at him, and then disappeared.

Raymond's parents noticed a great difference in his behavior from that time on. Much later, Mrs. Kolbe asked Raymond about this change, and he told her about Our Lady's visit to him.

The family attended a parish mission, and heard wonderful preaching about the Catholic Faith by Franciscan priests. At the end of the mission, the priests mentioned that a Franciscan seminary was being started in a nearby town. Lying in bed that night, Raymond prayed with all his might that he might be able to enter the seminary. He wanted with all his heart to be a Franciscan priest. He was glad to hear that his brother, Francis, wanted the same thing, too.

But many difficulties stood in the way. The family could not possibly afford tuition for two sons. Both boys also needed more education in order to enter. How could these difficulties be overcome?

The family prayed, and in time the difficulties seemed to solve themselves. With the tutoring help of a priest and a kind pharmacist, Raymond and his older brother, Francis, entered the Franciscan seminary high school in 1907. Raymond was a good student, and grew even closer to Our Lady. But in 1910, when the time came for him to enter the Franciscan order, following in the footsteps of St. Francis of Assisi, he hesitated. No, he had no doubts about wanting to be a priest and a Franciscan. But he remembered Our Lady's visit—he thought about it very often. How could

a Franciscan priest, living in a Catholic country in the 20th century, possibly be martyred for the Faith?

Raymond knew that one could be pure in any state of life—but how to die for God? He convinced himself that a soldier's life was for him. As a soldier, he could somehow die for the Faith. He even convinced his brother, Francis, to come with him! They both were just about to go to the room of their provincial, or superior, and tell him that they were leaving, when something happened. It was something very small, but it was about to change the life direction of both boys. What happened?

The doorbell rang! Both boys were called to the door. It was their mother! Mrs. Kolbe walked in, her face joyful.

"I have wonderful news! Your younger brother Joseph has also decided to become a Franciscan priest!" she said, tears of happiness in her eyes. As she told them more news of the family, Raymond came to a decision, and became very peaceful. He would follow God's Providence and become a Franciscan priest.

Many years later, he would write, "How can I ever forget that moment when Francis and I, awaiting an appointment with Father Provincial to tell him we did not wish to enter the Order, heard the bell ring in the reception room. At that very delicate moment the God of Providence, in His infinite mercy and through the services of Mary Immaculate, sent me my mother."

Shortly after this, Raymond entered the Franciscan Order and took a new name, as is a custom among religious. His name now was Maximilian. He never forgot the lesson of the doorbell, which was a lesson teaching him the meaning of God's Providence. Maximilian realized that the will of God makes itself known in the circumstances and happenings of our lives, and that obedience to his superiors would always guide him to do God's will.

Maximilian went to Rome to study. He learned the Latin word "Immaculata," meaning "one most pure and conceived without sin," which most perfectly described Our Lady. He used it all his life, and each day he grew in love and in appreciation of how God pours His Mercy on mankind through the heart of Our Lady. When he was ordained a priest in Rome in 1918, he said his first Mass in the church of Saint Andrea delle Fratte, at the altar where Our Lady converted Alphonse Ratisbonne, who had once been an enemy of God, through the Miraculous Medal.

This story could tell you about Fr. Kolbe founding the Militia of the Immaculata with only seven members who were pledged to convert and save souls by their consecration to Our Lady, asking to be used as an instrument in her hands, and wearing and giving away her Miraculous Medal. This story could tell you of the growth of the Militia, which today includes millions of men, women, and children. This story could tell you about the City of the Immaculata that Fr. Kolbe began from nothing, which grew into a giant complex of buildings with over six hundred Franciscans who printed Catholic magazines and newspapers by the thousands that were read all over Poland by people grateful for such wonderful articles about the Catholic Faith and Our Lady. This story could tell you about Fr. Kolbe traveling almost penniless to Japan, and working the same miracle there. But all that is food for another story.

Fr. Kolbe's writings attracted the attention of the Nazis. He fearlessly proclaimed the Faith, so he was arrested by the Nazi police, the Gestapo, in 1941. As he was riding to Auschwitz, perhaps he was thinking, "So this is the way I am to offer my life as a martyr. Thank you, my Immaculata, for keeping your promise to me that you made so long ago!"

Fr. Kolbe had this thought again as he saw the red sunset for the last time before entering the Bunker, reminding him of the red crown offered

to him so long ago. The prisoners gave up their clothes and shoes, and all ten were put in a windowless, airless, lightless, locked cement room underground, and were left to die of thirst and starvation. This was "The Bunker."

The guards would come in once a day to remove those who had died. Usually screams and moans were heard from the Bunker, because starvation is an agonizing way to die. But in Fr. Kolbe's Bunker could be heard the sounds of hymns and prayers, especially the prayer of the Rosary, started by Fr. Kolbe. He often started singing hymns to Our Lady, and all would join in, including condemned prisoners from other cells nearby.

This went on for two weeks. Fr. Kolbe comforted each man and helped him to die. The guards always saw him praying—sometimes he wouldn't even notice that they were there. "He is a real man! He is not like the others!" they said to each other.

A prisoner named Bruno Borgowiec was forced to accompany the guards, and to remove the dead. He survived Auschwitz, and remembered Fr. Kolbe well. We have him to thank for the story of Fr. Kolbe's last days.

"When I had to go down there, it was like descending into the crypt of a church. It was never like this before," he remembers. "In those days Fr. Kolbe displayed real heroism. He asked for nothing and never complained. He inspired the others with courage," he said many years later.

On August 14, the eve of that wonderful feast, the Assumption into Heaven of the Blessed Virgin Mary, Kommandant Fritsch ordered that the remaining prisoners of the bunker were to be killed, in order to make room for a new group. The camp doctor brought four syringes of phenol, one for each of the men remaining alive. One of the prisoners still alive was Fr. Kolbe.

The doctor injected the four men, and they died quickly. Bruno Borgowiec couldn't bear to watch them die, but he went into the Bunker shortly afterwards. He remembers, "When I opened the iron door, Fr. Kolbe was no longer alive. His face had an unusual radiance about it. The eyes were wide open and focused on some definite point. His entire person seemed to have been in a state of ecstasy. I will never forget that scene as long as I live." Perhaps Fr. Kolbe was seeing the loving face of his beloved Immaculata, who had come to take him home!

On October 10, 1982, St. John Paul II canonized Fr. Maximilian Kolbe as a martyr, and called him "the patron saint of our difficult century." His life was to prove true his favorite motto: "Love alone creates."

Show Your Faith!

At the present time in this country we are blessed that we do not have to hide our Catholic Faith the way Bl. Miguel Pro and St. Maximilian Kolbe had to. Even so, sometimes it is hard to resist the temptation to "go with the flow." Create a T-shirt, tote bag, bumper sticker, or book cover with a slogan expressing some aspect of the values you hold dear as a Catholic. If you design a T-shirt, you can paint your design with fabric paints, machine stitch your message onto fabric, or even have your message applied to multiple T-shirts by a screen printing company. You can use the blank T-shirt on the next page to practice with, before applying your design. Use the ideas below to jump-start your own creative ideas.

If God is all you have
You have all you need.
(Matt. 6:33)

"A dead thing can go with the stream,
but only a living thing can go against it."
—G.K. Chesterton

"Those who stand for nothing
fall for anything."
—Alexander Hamilton

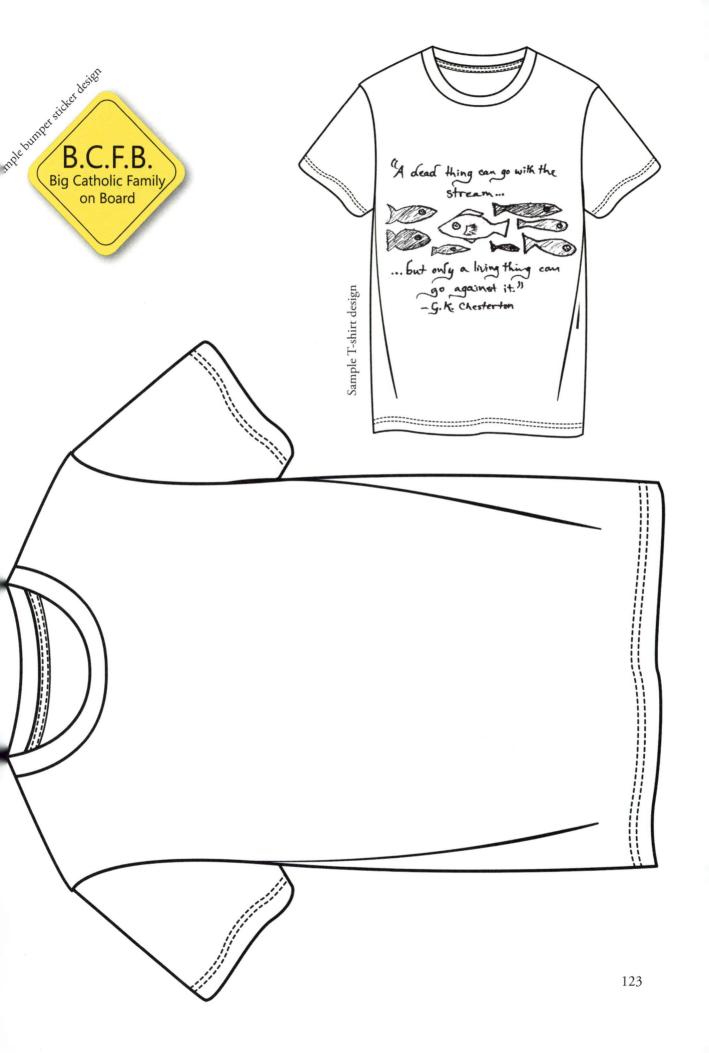

B.C.F.B.
Big Catholic Family
on Board

Sample T-shirt design

"A dead thing can go with the stream...

...but only a living thing can go against it."
– G. K. Chesterton

18–21 | Personal Prayer Book

To grow our relationship with God it is important to open ourselves to His love each day. Over the next several weeks you will be creating your own personal prayer book. Use the prayer book as a tool to help your mind and heart "tune in" as you begin your prayers. Some days you will be brimming with thanks and adoration, other days it may be contrition and petition. Offer all your good actions and thoughts to God, and ask Him for the necessary grace to do His will.

First, cut out all the blank prayer pages on pages 127–148. Store them in an envelope to protect their edges. Then choose a verse, prayer, or saint quote that you like from the ones provided and write it neatly on the front of one of the blank prayer pages. You can also choose your own prayers and use colored paper if you don't care for the images provided. On the back of each prayer page, write out a one-liner from the list provided on page 126 to inspire you in practical ways. When you have completed your prayer book, laminate the pages for durability and hole punch.

Scripture Verses * Prayers * Saint Quotes

His tender and loving gaze is upon me.

Guide me, Lord, along the everlasting way.

You are precious in My eyes, and I love you. (Isaiah 43:4)

Dear Jesus, take my heart and let it be A little holy altar just for Thee.

My God, I desire to do and to endure everything today for love of Thee. —St. Bernadette

Your holy will: nothing more, nothing less, nothing else.

Enlighten and empower me to do Your will.

Dear God, I offer You today everything I do a say, that I may be in some small part united t Your Sacred Heart.

Please give me what I ask, dear Lord,
If You'd be glad about it,
But if You think it's not for me,
Please help me do without it. Amen.

Beautiful angel!
My guardian so mild,
Tenderly guide me,
For I am your child.

He died, but He vanquished death; in Himself
He put an end to what we feared; He took
it upon Himself and He vanquished it, as a
mighty hunter He captured and slew the lion.
—St. Augustine

Dear Jesus, I offer to you my body and
my soul; all that I am and all I have.
My thoughts, my desires, my words, my
actions, and my whole being are Yours.

For I, the Lord your God,
hold your right hand;
it is I who say to you, "Fear not,
I will help you." (Isaiah 41:13)

Day by day, dear Lord of Thee
Three things I pray:
To serve Thee more clearly,
To love Thee more dearly,
To follow Thee more nearly,
Day by day. —St. Richard

O Lord, You are my Father;
I am the clay and You the potter;
I am the work of Your hands. (Isaiah 64:7)

Baby Jesus smiling sweet
On Your Mother's knee,
I am opening wide my heart,
Won't you come to me?

I am only one, but I am one. I cannot do
everything, but I can do something. What
I can do, I ought to do, and what I ought
to do, by the grace of God, I will do.
—Dr. Tom Dooley

I like to think the days are steps
On which You've set my feet,
And I must climb them one by one,
Dear God, until we meet.
—Mary Dixon Thayer

Be afraid neither of the world, nor of the
future, nor of your weakness. The Lord
has allowed you to live in this moment of
history so that, by your faith, His name will
continue to resound throughout the world.
—Benedict XVI

God, make my life a little light,
Within the world to glow;
A tiny flame that burneth bright
Wherever I may go.
—Matilda Betham-Edwards

Lord of the loving heart,
May mine be loving too.
Lord of the gentle hands,
May mine be gentle too.
Lord of the willing feet,
May mine be willing too.
So I may grow more like Thee
In all I say and do.

Come to me sweet Savior,
Come to me and stay,
For I love Thee, Jesus,
More than I can say.

One-Liners

God loves each of us as if there were only one of us. —St. Augustine

Heaven—don't miss it for the world.

I will not leave you or forsake you. (Josiah 1:5)

Backsliding begins when knee-bending ends.

He has given you a way to follow, so stick to Him. —St. Augustine

Love alone creates. —St. Maximilian Kolbe

Prayer is powerful, it fills the earth with mercy. — Mother Cabrini

Be not anxious about what you have, but about what you are.

A cheerful spirit gets on quick; a grumbler in the mud will stick.

Give Satan an inch and he'll be a ruler.

My blessed task from day to day is nobly, gladly to obey.

It is well to be wise and great; 'tis better to be good.

Good unites. Evil divides.

Jesus my Savior, You are in my heart and I am in Your hands.

Lord, please help me not to get in Your way, but to stay with You on the Way.

I can do all things in Him who strengthens me. (Philippians 4:13)

Give God what's right—not what's left.

Don't put a question mark where God puts a period.

Exercise daily—walk with the Lord.

Never give the devil a ride—he will always want to drive.

Nothing else ruins the truth like stretching it.

Pointing a finger at another leaves three fingers pointing back at me.

Often repeat with St. Paul, "Lord, what will You have me to do?"—St. John Bosco

For where your treasure is, there will your heart be also. (Matthew 6:21)

Prayer Pages

128

135